Ghosts of NY's Capital District

Albany * Amsterdam * Clifton Park * Cohoes * Glens Falls * Menands
* Rensselaer * Saratoga Springs * Schenectady * Scotia * Stillwater * Troy

D1503029

Renee Mallett

4880 Lower Valley Road, Atglen, Pennsylvania 19310

Dedication

This book is dedicated to my Dad,
who has always known all the best stories.

Cover image: New York State Capitol Building At Night © Wayne Archembeault.
Photo courtesy of bigstockphotos.com.

Schiffer Books are available at special discounts for bulk purchases for sales promotions or premiums. Special editions, including personalized covers, corporate imprints, and excerpts can be created in large quantities for special needs. For more information contact the publisher:

Published by Schiffer Publishing Ltd.
4880 Lower Valley Road
Atglen, PA 19310
Phone: (610) 593-1777; Fax: (610) 593-2002
E-mail: Info@schifferbooks.com

For the largest selection of fine reference books on this and related subjects, please visit our web site at
www.schifferbooks.com
We are always looking for people to write books on new and related subjects.
If you have an idea for a book please contact us at the above address.

This book may be purchased from the publisher.
Include $5.00 for shipping.
Please try your bookstore first.
You may write for a free catalog.

In Europe, Schiffer books are distributed by
Bushwood Books
6 Marksbury Ave.
Kew Gardens
Surrey TW9 4JF England
Phone: 44 (0) 20 8392 8585; Fax: 44 (0) 20 8392 9876
E-mail: info@bushwoodbooks.co.uk
Website: www.bushwoodbooks.co.uk

Other Schiffer Books by Renee Mallett:
Manchester Ghosts. ISBN: 978-0-7643-2650-9. $14.95

Copyright © 2009 by Renee Mallett
Library of Congress Control Number: 2009922318

Designed by Mark David Bowyer
Type set in Berylium / Zurich BT

ISBN: 978-0-7643-3292-0
Printed in the United States of America

Contents

Author's Note

This is a book of real-life ghost stories and other paranormal or otherwise unexplainable occurrences. The stories are based on first-person accounts, and some of the cases are quite famous and have been reported online and in other books, newspapers, or magazines. Many of the stories, like all great ghost stories, have an element of local legend or folklore to them, and they walk the thin line between fiction and fact.

This book would not exist without the generosity of the people who have decided to shared their experiences and, as the old saying goes, many of the names have been changed to protect the identity of the people involved. Some business names have been altered or addresses not given in order to protect their privacy.

Please keep in mind that all of the places written about in this book are real places that offer you, the reader, the opportunity to go and visit yourself. That being said, these places are private residences, places of business, abandoned buildings, or places of education, etc. Please use common sense and a good healthy dose of self-interest before going to any of these places. Abandoned buildings are usually left empty for a reason, they may be filled with asbestos, and they might be structurally unsound. You might also want to keep in mind that real living human beings have caused more injuries and assaults than any number of ghosts ever could. Before visiting any un-abandoned haunted site remember that the living people in these places deserve respect and privacy first and foremost. Exact house numbers and street names are not given for any of the private homes in this book. Never trespass on other people's property; always get permission before you decide to go ghost hunting and decide to visit a haunted site. All would be ghost hunters are legally responsible for their own actions. Be careful and be safe.

There are many walking tours that make the rounds to haunted sites, particularly in the month of October. Local libraries and historical societies often host 'ghost nights' in legendary buildings in town as part of their Halloween events. These ghost tours and lectures are an ideal, safe, and legal way to experience haunted places and ghostly phenomena yourself, usually for nothing more than a modest admission fee and without taking on the added risk and expense of a trespassing charge.

Acknowledgments

Both my grandmother and my great aunt lent me books on local Capital District history from their own bookshelves that I would never have been able to find on my own. So, Ann Flagg and Joyce Bordeau should be credited for helping to add a great deal of information about the history of the region to this book.

I am deeply indebted to Jennifer Sack and Lisa Lavery who were both kind enough to take time out of their own busy schedules and take some pictures for me to include in this book.

As always, none of my books would exist if it weren't for Dinah Roseberry (who fixes all my mistakes) and the team at Schiffer Books. The book writing process wouldn't be half as much fun, and not nearly as satisfying, if it wasn't done with the help and support of all those fine people down in Pennsylvania. I also owe many thanks to the booksellers who do the actual work of getting these books into the hands of the people who read them.

Introduction

Ask anyone is the area what the Capital District is and you'll get a lot of very different responses. Purists will tell you that it is strictly the cities of Schenectady, Albany, and Troy. A growing number of people will include Saratoga with those three cities. Others will include any of the smaller towns and hamlets in-between those cities. Still others will say only towns within Albany County . . . or any place within the Albany, Schenectady, Rensselaer and Saratoga Counties . . . or anyplace that is in the 518 area code . . . or, well, you get the idea. There are just about as many distinctions as you can imagine and probably a lot that you can't.

For the purposes of this book, and with the goal of being as all inclusive as possible, some people may not be happy with some of the cities I decided to include. An equal number of people will be upset with some of the cities I decided to leave out. In the end I am a storyteller before all else so the two most important guidelines for me were A) to tell interesting stories I thought people would like to hear and B) to give the most complete picture of the different types of haunting that can be found in this general area of upstate New York.

Albany

Albany is the capital of New York state and the county seat of Albany County, so it is considered to be the heart of the Capital District. It is the second oldest state capital in the United States, just behind Santa Fe, and its long history makes it a great spot to find historic hauntings and ghostly specters of days gone by.

Lincoln's Ghost Train

The old fashioned train moves slowly, silently, up the tracks. It pulls only nine Pullman cars behind it, the windows thronged with 300 faces obscured behind black drapes. They are as eerily silent as the train itself, simply looking forlornly from the windows, seeing nothing of the landscape around them. Everywhere along the outside of the train black flags stream back sadly into the night air. Silvery grey puffs of smoke stream from the engine stack. In one of the cars you see dozens of blue suited men standing in a silent vigil over an ornate coffin. Suddenly the stark sad sounds of a bell toll. In an instant the train has passed, swallowed by the night ahead on the tracks, and if you watch carefully you may see the name *The Union* scrawled along one side.

This strange train is one of the eeriest and most well known American haunting. Each April it has been reported everywhere from Washington D.C. to Springfield, Illinois and throughout Upstate New York. It has been seen often just outside of Albany on the track line known for time out of mind as the New York Central. It is said to be the ghostly remnant of the very real train that once carried the body of President Abraham Lincoln to Springfield for burial.

Lincoln was the 16th President of the United States and, by most accounts, one of the most successful and iconic. He is famous for being an outspoken opponent to expanding the practice of slavery throughout the country and led the nation to reunite after the Civil War. His Gettysburg Address, given after the extremely bloody Battle of Gettysburg, is one of the most recognizable speeches in American history.

Lincoln also holds the dubious honor of being the first United States President to be assassinated. On April 14, 1865 Lincoln and his wife went to Ford's Theatre to see the comedic play *Our American Cousin*. At the moment the play's most humorous line was delivered an actor, and sometime Confederate spy, John Wilkes Booth snuck up behind the President and shot him once in the head. Shouting "Sic Semper Tyrannis!" (*Thus always to tyrants!*) Booth leapt to the stage, breaking his leg in the prog-ress, and still managed to escape. Twelve days later he would be found hiding in Virginia and would be killed before he could ever be brought to trial.

Lincoln did not last nearly so long. After being shot he re-mained in a coma for nine hours and died without awakening. Lincoln's body was placed in a casket and traveled, by train, from Washington D.C to Springfield Illinois via a circuitous route that took it throughout New York State. Everywhere the black draped train went the tracks were lined with mourners. In Springfield the body was interred in the Oak Ridge Cemetery.

In life Lincoln was immensely interested in the supernatural. He is the only President known to have hosted séances in the White House. Lincoln even, rather famously, predicted his own death. So, perhaps, it should not be surprising that Lincoln's ghost has been reported many times, in dozens of different locations, since his assassination. Lincoln's ghost has been seen in Fort Monroe, Virginia, walking around his grave in Springfield, and even in the White House itself. The Presidents ghost awaked Queen Wilhelmina of the Netherlands one evening when she was a guest in the Lincoln Room of the White House. Jacqueline Kennedy Onassis, Eleanor Roosevelt, and Teddy Roosevelt all reported sensing or seeing Lincoln's ghost while living in the White House. The spirit is even said to have driven Franklin Delano Roosevelt's dog, Fala, to distraction. During the dogs time living in the White House many people said they saw the animal look up, chase, and bark excitedly at something no human could see.

But the most widely reported Lincoln spirit is that of his funeral train. Towards the end of April each year along the path the train followed witness after witness reports similar phenomena. The air on either side of the train tracks may be warm but above the tracks itself the air is ice cold. Watches stop when the train passes by, batteries on cell phones and MP3 players are mysteriously drained of power, and sometimes-ghostly piano music can be heard. But, of course, the most haunting specter is that of the train itself, rising up out of the ether for a brief glimpse, before fading away into the night again. If a real train happens to be on the same track as the ghost train goes by the noise of the real train is overpowered by the silence as the ghost train engulfs it before passing by.

There is even at least one known account of the ghost train passing over a human. One cold April many years ago a conductor stopped his train when he saw something on the tracks. He sent a railroad man to investigate. While the man was busy clearing the track of brush he felt a frigid wind slam into him. Looking up he got one look at the looming black train before it was on top of him. The man didn't even have time to scream.

His eyes wide with fright he saw only a wave of the blackest black he could imagine fall over him like a wave. As he stood there paralyzed in the frigid cold the tracks began to glow an unearthly blue and his lantern was snuffed out. Somehow he was able to break though the darkness and fell to the side of the tracks. Looking up he saw the tail end of an old fashioned train passing straight through his train. It was gone in an instant. When he returned to his train he quietly questioned the other workers but no one had seen what he had, although a few commented on a sudden cold snap that had inexplicably passed through the train while he was outside clearing the tracks.

University of Albany, State University of New York

University of Albany, or U of A as this college is commonly called, is a public university that was founded in 1844, as the State Normal School. It did not receive its current name until 1986. University of Albany has three campuses; the uptown and downtown campuses are located within the city of Albany and another campus is found in East Greenbush.

There are more than 17,000 students attending University of Albany in any given school year and more than a few of them have reported seeing ghosts on the schools campus.

Paige Hall

Paige Hall is the site of one of the University of Albany's most mundane, but longest running, spirits. A ghostly figure has been observed for more than fifteen years walking around and throughout the building. The ghost is distinct enough that several of the more long-term employees have been able to recognize him! The spirit is that of a former security guard, one who, long after death, is still making his rounds and watching out for U of A's student body.

The Humanities Building

The Humanities Building is quiet and spook free- during the day at least! Night is an entirely different story. The spirit in the Humanities Building is, in many ways, like a poltergeist, except that activity is centered around this building instead of around a person. It spends the evening hours turning lights on and off, slamming doors, and moving objects from one room to another. One former janitor swears that not only did this ghost use to hide his keys but that he also saw objects disappear right before his very eyes.

Mohican Hall

The ghost of Mohican Hall is shrouded in mystery and de-bate. The ghost was not sensed in the building until 1994, lead-ing some to speculate that the spirit is linked to one or another tragedy that befell a student that year. The only problem is that if there was a tragedy no one seems to know exactly what it could be. Does this mean that the ghost of Mohican Hall is just a figment of the students over active imaginations?

It is not uncommon for previously un-haunted buildings or places to become haunted. Ghosts are usually very stodgy and set in their ways. They like things to remain quiet and to remain the same, two things not often found on a college campus with thousands of students wandering around and new people arriv-ing every year. Construction or remodeling projects have been known to stir up ghostly activity where before there was none. In some cases people have been besieged by supernatural activity just because they rearranged their furniture in a way that their resident spirit didn't care for. So it is possible that the ghost of Mohican Hall is simply an unusual side effect of an otherwise commonplace maintenance project.

On top of this ghosts also are known for traveling, a fact that surprises many people. Ghosts are very attached to what is familiar to them. If their current residence no longer feels comfortable to them they sometimes move, usually relatively short distances, until they find a building that looks more like the time period they are use to. As old buildings have been torn down or remodeled in any given neighborhood owners of a home that has been restored to be historically accurate suddenly find they are housing several new ghosts.

Pierce Hall

Ladies in white, or ladies in grey or ladies in black as they are sometimes described, are probably the second most common type of ghostly entity, right behind orb photography. Sightings of white ladies have been reported around the world, in one form or another, for almost as long as we have written records. They are usually tragic figures. They have been betrayed by a lover, have lost a beloved fiancée, or are mothers whose children were taken from her or killed. In many places white ladies are associated with a specific family and these ladies are signs that someone in the family is about to die. In this way they seem to be closely related to banshees, who belong to Irish folklore. But it is equally common for a white lady to be linked to a building or stretch of road as it is for her to be associated with a specific family.

Though these lady ghosts inevitably appear at scenes of great tragedy, they are not said to be frightening specters at all. Most often witnesses report seeing the women crying or feeling waves of sadness emanating from them. The lady ghost is seen in dresses of white, hence the name, usually of an old fashioned cut. Most often the white lady is seen in Victorian garb, perhaps having something to do with the fact that there was a keen interest in the spiritualist movement during the same time period in the United States. White ladies either act out scenes of their own tragedies, unaware of the passage of time or that they are caught in a loop of memory they cannot break out of, or they act as a warning to the witness. White ladies sometimes reveal themselves to someone destined to die, or a friend of someone destined to die, but at least a few stories credit them with giving the warning that allows the witness to cheat fate.

The United States has a plethora of famous white lady hauntings. A woman in an old fashioned white dress visits the Old Faithful Inn in Yellowstone Park nightly. The legend says she was the daughter of a wealthy merchant who fell in love with a servant boy and ran off to elope. The young couple honeymooned at the Old Faithful Inn but theirs was not a story that would end with 'happily ever after'. The young man was a scoundrel and compulsive gambler. Soon he had frittered away the little bit of money the couple had, leaving them with no way to pay their hotel room bill and with no place else to go. The young woman, desperate, called the father she had just fled from and asked for a loan. The father refused. When the husband found out his young bride was unable to bail him out of the mess he had made he killed her in a fit of rage, beheading her, and fleeing into the night never to be seen again. Since that time the young lady appears at midnight, still clothed in the wedding dress that was supposed to symbolize a brand new start for her, and holding her head in the crook of her arm. She walks slowly around the hotel, looking to see if her young man has decided to return to her. When she realizes he has not she slowly fades away.

This story from Yellowstone can be heard, with some variations, around the country. Every state has at least one famous white lady and most have a handful. New York is no different and one of these lady ghosts haunts Pierce Hall. The white lady of Pierce Hall is unique in the fact that no one seems to know her tragic story and, even more surprisingly, if anyone has ever tried to make one up for her it's never caught on. Dozens of students and employees of the college have seen her over the years, walking aimlessly around Pierce Hall and a few times around the Alumni Quad. Whatever her purpose, to find a lost love, to relieve a memory, or to warn of danger to come, it is as mysterious as her origins.

Performing Arts Center

The spirit located in the Performing Arts Center is most often described as an 'eerie presence'. At night common complaints are doors that are locked, or unlocked, when they shouldn't be, doors that lock immediately after they are unlocked, doors that slam open and shut by themselves, and doors that refuse to open at all. Some feel that the incidents are more malicious than a simple prank. No matter what your take on the intent almost everyone can agree the actions of this ghost are annoying.

Some people have reported closer encounters with the ghost at the Performing Arts Center. Some have heard the sound of heavy footsteps walking back and forth where there was no one to be seen. This pacing is often accompanied by the sound of jangling keys, like those a janitor or maintenance worker might carry. A rare few have actually seen the figure of a maintenance worker walking around the building. His face is completely missing, a strange blurred visage that is lacking eyes, a mouth, or nose.

This ghost is known as Andi Lyons. The story goes that he was a maintenance worker at the school who died by electrocution while working on a problem in the Performing Arts Center.

The Capitol Building

When the New York State capitol building was constructed it was the single most expensive government building of its time. It was built at the cost of $25 million dollars. Bear in mind that is $25 million in 19th century money, taking inflation into account, that is roughly equivalent to half a billion dollars in today's currency. The building took over thirty years to complete. The capitol building was based heavily on the Hotel de Ville in Paris, France and is a unique blend of Renaissance and Romanesque architectural styles, which has led to its "Battle of the Styles" moniker.

Even before the building was completed it was the scene of several tragedies. Workers on the building seemed to get injured more often than construction workers on other spaces. Even the quarry in Hallowell, Maine that supplied the white granite that makes up the outside of the building reported a higher incident of injuries during the time they were cutting stone for use on the capitol building. In 1887 one of these giant blocks of stone would slide from its place in the ceiling and nearly kill an Assemblyman who had come to see the progress on the building. After the building opened the slew of accidents slowed but never stopped entirely.

On March 29, 1911, in the early morning hours, while the capitol building was empty, a great fire occurred. At this time the New York State library was housed in the building along with the assembly and it was decimated in the blaze. Many have called it one of the greatest library disasters of modern times. Half a million books and another quarter million manuscripts were lost in the blaze, many of them one of a kind and completely irreplaceable. Some blamed the fire of a smoldering cigar left behind by a careless Assemblyman. Others blamed the electrical system. No satisfactory explanation ever came forward to explain the blaze.

The most active ghost in the capitol building is on the fifth floor. This spirit has been nicknamed George by the State workers who are employed in the building. George makes his presence known by jingling an invisible set of keys and fiddling with doorknobs throughout the fifth floor. Shadows are said to move around this floor and sometimes, out of the corner of your eye, these shadows seem to take the shape of men.

In 1981 a psychic visited the capitol building and was able to give a name to the spirit everyone called George. The psychic said the ghost's true name was Samuel Abbott and that he had been a night watchman who died in the 1911 fire. If Sam Abbott is the ghost who haunts the ol Building having his true name learned was not enough to quiet him down. This has led to some speculation that perhaps Samuel Abbott was the cause of the fire and his spirit is trapped at the scene because of some kind of guilt. It is also just as possible that if he died in the blaze he feels the need to stay on and protect others from a similar fate.

The interesting thing is that the fire destroyed, mainly, the third and fourth floors of the building, which were completely given over to the library's use. But the ghostly activity of 'George' is confined almost entirely to the fifth floor. So it seems possible that the haunting at the capitol building has nothing to do with the fire at all and that the ghost dates to a different time for an entirely different reason.

The College of Saint Rose

The College of Saint Rose was begun in 1920 as a Roman Catholic college for women only. Today the school is co-ed and, while it strives to respect its Roman Catholic beginnings, has become an institution of learning for students of all faiths. It is one of several schools in the Capital District that has signed a pledge to reduce their carbon footprint and become more environmentally friendly.

College campuses tend to be popular spots for ghost sightings. Typical stories involve fires, suicides, accidents, or murders that happened at some unspecified time way back in the college's history that there is no current evidence of. The College of Saint Rose is unique in the fact that its myths and legends are of the more verifiable variety.

The College of Saint Rose began as a Roman Catholic college for girls.
Photo courtesy of Jennifer Sack

Morris Hall

When the college was a convent for the sisters of Saint Mercy Morris Hall was used as a chapel. The ghost here seems to date from this time. For many years students reported seeing the spirit of a priest wandering around Morris Hall's common room. Several years ago there was a renovation project that subdivided the common room into two smaller spaces and since that time the ghost has been silent.

This is an unusual occurrence to say the least. Normally renovation projects seem to stir ghosts up. Houses that were previously as un-haunted as you could imagine suddenly have joke playing ghosts hiding tools or bossy spirits who try to make their tastes in wall color and curtains known. There are very few reports of building projects that stop ghostly occurrences from happening. Yet that seems to be exactly what has happened in Morris Hall. Perhaps several years down the road the college will alter this building again and their ghostly priest will return to them.

This former chapel used to be home to a ghostly priest.
Photo courtesy of Lisa Lavery

Carey Hall

There are several different stories about the ghosts in Carey Hall. They have been identified as everything from the spirit of a Mother who hangs around the house since her child died in the house as an infant, a man who enjoys gardening, a little girl, and a man who grew up in Carey Hall while it was still a private residence that died after going off to war. It is unclear if these ghosts might be related to each other or why the house is such a spirit hot spot.

Carey Hall is home to a multitude of ghosts including a soldier, a small girl, and a grieving mother.
Photo Courtesy of Lisa Lavery

Carey Hall's ghosts are not seen as frightening in any way. They act more like protective elements; they loved the house in life and stayed on after death because this is where they felt the happiest. More than anything they want their presence recognized. One Resident Assistant recounts the story about a shade flying up at the precise moment she was telling a new student about the ghost stories, as if one of the ghosts was trying to 'prove' their presence in Carey Hall.

Quillinan Hall

Quillinan Hall is also home to the spirit of a little girl. When this home was still a private residence there was a devastating fire in the basement that may have been set by the owner's small daughter. The child died in the blaze. Students in this building have seen and interacted with the little girl since the building has become property of the college. She walks around the building playing jacks and asking students if they'd like to play with her. No word yet from anyone who has taken the ghost up on her offer.

Quillinan Hall, like other College of Saint Rose residence halls, is shared with a ghostly little girl. *Photo courtesy of Lisa Lavery*

Unlike a lot of ghost sightings that are blamed on a horrific fire or other disaster from a long ago time the Quillinan building actually shows some evidence that, at one point, there was basement fire here. During a renovation project workers found that the underside of the staircase, previously inaccessible, was charred and covered with soot.

During renovations workers found evidence that backs up the story associated with the ghostly little girl of Quillinan Hall. *Photo courtesy of Lisa Lavery*

The Murder at Cherry Hill

Elsie was not, by most accounts, what a man in the early 1800s dreamed of in a wife. She was known for her outrageous temper, her uncontrollable hysterics, and her violent screaming fits. She was, however, the only daughter of Abraham Lansing and Elsie Van Rensselaer, both from prominent Albany families. So while Elsie's charm may have lacked her inheritance certainly did not and so it is not too surprising that, even with her fiery contentious reputation, she managed to snag a husband pretty easily. But, as it is probably just as easy to guess, married life did nothing to settle the head strong Elsie. Much of her anger turned towards her husband, John Whipple, who she saw as a domineering and controlling man.

In 1826 Elsie met Joseph Orten while out at an Albany bar. In a surprisingly short amount of time Elsie and Joseph decided they were in love and had to be together at all costs. Elsie managed to get him a job as a handyman at her own home, Cherry Hill Farm. Servants at Cherry Hill Farm did their part to keep the lovers in contact, hiding their indiscretions and smuggling love notes between the two.

There were a few things about Elsie's inamorato she did not know. He was not, in fact, Joseph Orten at all. Nor was he a native of Ohio. He was Jesse Strang, a New Yorker, who had abandoned his wife and child and taken off for a life of adventure. His adventures only ever brought him as far as Ohio. There he would run out of money and decide to head back to New York. It was only by the bad luck of some misdirected luggage that he ended up in Albany instead of his hometown.

Elsie wanted to be free of her husband. His so called controlling behavior certainly was helped along by the fact that he started to suspect something was going on between his wife and their new handyman. It seemed, Elsie reasoned, the only way to ever be free of the man was to kill him and run off to

Montreal with 'Joseph Orten'. There is much evidence that the murder plot was Elsie's idea entirely and one can't help but think that if Jesse had just run off from one marriage he probably wasn't in a hurry to jump right into another, especially one with a murderess who had already left one marriage a widow. But Elsie got her way, as she almost always did. Their first attempt at murder involved a cup of tea heavily dosed with arsenic. But either their dosage calculation was off or John Whipple was a little more suspicious of them than they expected that night because the next morning he was still perfectly healthy and wandering around Cherry Hill Farm.

That was it. Elsie was done with subtleties. That night she pulled the curtains from the windows in her husband's room, telling him they needed cleaning, and handed her lover a loaded rifle. A, by most accounts, reluctant Jesse climbed up on the roof of the house and shot John Whipple dead.

In a flash Jesse was off the roof and in a mad dash to the closest store to establish an alibi. As soon as he felt like he was seen by enough people, he returned to Cherry Hill Farm to help the police with the clean up. And, at first, the police believed him. Plenty of people had seen Jesse in the store around the same time some mysterious figure was on the roof shooting the prominent local farmer. They certainly didn't look twice at Elsie as a suspect. What woman would kill her own husband? But enough people knew about the affair to cloud the pristine image of the grieving 19th century housewife that Elsie was trying to portray and the police started taking a closer look at things. It didn't take much figuring to realize that Jesse easily could have shot John Whipple and run the mile through the woods to the store. Shortly after the crime Jesse Strang was picked up by the police on suspicion of murder.

His false name blown, and with the prospect of facing his abandoned wife and a murder charge at the same time Jesse confessed. But there was, it seemed, no honor among criminals. Figuring he could get a lighter sentence if he played the hopeless dupe Jesse blamed the entire thing on Elsie. When Elsie was picked up on suspicion of murder she blamed the entire thing on the love of her life, Jesse. The police were left with two feuding lovers, hurling accusations at each other, and one dead body.

Jesse couldn't understand why Elsie wouldn't take the blame. He was sure a woman would get a lighter sentence. Elsie was furious that Jesse had ever confessed in the first place. If he had just kept his mouth shut, she reasoned, they would be living the high life in Montreal right now.

It took a jury less than fifteen minutes to declare Jesse Strang guilty and sentence him to death. He was to be kept alive just long enough to stand witness at the trial of his former lover, Elsie. In less than a week a jury of her peers heard all the evidence, including the testimony of Jesse himself, and found Elsie not guilty of any crime. Jesse had been right about one thing, if nothing else; a woman would not be seen as being as guilty as a man.

On August 24, 1827 Jesse Strang was executed in Albany for the crime of murder. It would be the last public hanging to take place in the city. Elsie returned to Cherry Hill Farm and lived out the rest of her days there, in the same home where her husband was murdered. The crime was a sensation at the time and among crime history buffs it is controversial to this day. Today, just as in the 1820s, there are as many people who believe Elsie was the victim in the situation as believe she was the mastermind. Was justice served, or justice denied, to John Whipple? It is unlikely that we will ever know for sure.

Today Cherry Hill Farm is known as Historic Cherry Hill and has been a public museum since 1964. Having belonged to five generations of the Van Rensselaer family the house is a unique look at the changing fortunes of both the distinguished family and the community around them. Historic Cherry Hill is definitely a place where the past lives on, for both better and worse. Intermixed with the historic photographs and antiques some visitors feel a ghostly presence that many feel is linked to the murder of John Whipple.

The ghost is always described as a male presence, whether it is actually seen or just sensed. It tends to keep to the lower floor of the home. But no one has been able to say for sure if the spirit is that of murdered John Whipple or that of executed, and some might argue betrayed, Jesse Strang. The ghost is not frightening but it certainly seems to carry an atmosphere of anger around it. But is it the anger of someone spurned by his wife and shot by her lover or the anger of someone who was punished for a crime they did not want to commit, even while they watched the true mastermind walk free?

Historic Cherry Hill is located at 523½ South Pearl Street and can found online at HistoricCherryHill.org.

The Dungeon of the New York State Education Building

You probably wouldn't think that a place popularly known as 'the dungeon' would be in the New York State Education building. But if you saw the sub-basement of this building you'd certainly see where the moniker came from. The basement alone is a creepy eerie place, few people know about the elevator shaft that can bring you to the far deeper and far creepier sub basement. Surprisingly there are some workers whose jobs take them down to these gloomy depths quite often in the course of their day-to-day work and the stories they sometimes bring back are enough to have built up many layers of local legend around the place.

Usually on a new employee's first day at work in the Education Building they are introduced to the most persistent legend about the dungeon. When the cement was being laid for the sub basement foundation a worker went missing. Many assumed he simply walked off the job for reasons of his own. He may have taken a lunch break that dragged on a little too long and, rather than try to explain his absence, chose to leave the worksite for good. Later on this workers lunch box and house keys would be found. This has led, all these years later, to speculation that perhaps the worker had somehow fallen into the wet cement foundation and been unable to extract himself. It certainly seems a little too urban legend-ish to be true but oftentimes in even in the most outlandish of local legends there is a grain or two of truth in there somewhere. Over the years storytellers have even given a name to this (probably entirely fictitious) construction worker, Jason.

As the spirit of the sub-basement Jason is said to like to attach himself to the people who are sometimes sent to find something in the old books or documents that are stored down there. These unlucky folks spend their time in the dungeon surrounded by a chill they can't shake, regardless of the true temperature of the room. While their colleagues walk around perfectly comfortable in short sleeves or skirts the very breath of these unfortunate employees can be see as plumes of frost.

As employees come and go Jason comes along behind them switching on the lights they have just turned off. For a ghost he doesn't seem to enjoy the dark very much. Many employees have ended up stuck in the sub-basement much longer than they planned, switching off the lights every time they go to leave, only to have to keep switching them off since Jason keeps turning them on every time the elevator appears.

That is not to say that Jason is a nuisance for most workers. He is legendary for helping people find whatever they have been sent downstairs to retrieve. Workers have spent hours digging through piles of old books only to hear a crash come from the unexplored, and empty, portion of the dungeon. When they go to investigate they find the very book they have been looking for, laying on the floor, as though someone unseen pushed it from the shelf.

Jason seems, if anything, lonely. He is extremely interested in anyone who comes down to the sub-basement. Almost everyone reports feeling as though someone is looking over their shoulder as they work down in the dungeon. A few have even thought they've seen the figure of a man out of the corner of their eye as they work. When they turn their head to greet the intruder they find the room empty.

Amsterdam

Fire Station Number 4

I n the 1970s it was common for there to only be two firefight-ers working on any given night in Fire Station #4, located at the corner of Bunn and Chestnut Streets. John had been working the station for many years and preferred the night shift. When things were quiet, and generally they were, the firefight-ers would take turns sleeping through the late hours. John was so used to the creaks and settling of the building that he liked to joke he was more comfortable sleeping in his bed upstairs there than the bed in his own home.

But one evening his sleep was disturbed, not by the fire alarm or a frantic phone call, but by the sounds of someone mov-ing stealthily through the fire stations sleeping quarters. John passed it off as his partner coming up to catch some sleep and rolled over to get more comfortable. But when he rolled over he was confronted with the view of his partner's bunk- with his fellow firefighter already in bed sound asleep!

At that very moment John heard loud footsteps rush towards his bedside. Convinced that an intruder had broken into the fire station he tried to leap up from the bunk. To his surprise he found he could not move a muscle. Above him a misty white figure loomed over his bed, holding him down with one nearly transparent hand. He could feel a stabbing cold emanating from the figure and where it touched his skin to hold him down felt icy. He tried to call for help and wake up his fellow firefighter but could not utter even the slightest noise. Whether that was from fear or from some sort of hold the ghost had over him he could never say.

As quickly as the spirit had appeared it vanished, backing up quickly and disappearing through a brick wall. John jumped up from the bunk with no problem now that the figure was gone. He would never see the ghost again but one thing was for sure, he no longer liked working the night shift at fire station #4.

Green Hill Cemetery

Green Hill Cemetery, located at the corners of Church and Cornell Street, may just be the single best place in Amsterdam, if not the entire ol District, to take spirit photographs. Many photographers, even those not hoping for a little proof of life after death, have walked away from this cemetery with images filled with strange streaks of bright color and dozens of orbs.

When most people think of ghost photos they imagine a misty sort of figure floating above the air, dressed in period clothes. It is actually extremely rare to get a full-bodied apparition like that on film. In fact it is so rare that most paranormal investigators automatically assume any such images are fakes. The most common photo you'll get that shows spirit activity is these orb photos. Orbs are small, faintly fuzzy looking blobs that sometimes show up in photos when they could not be seen in real life. Most often they are a dirty whitish-grey color, although it is not unheard of to get greenish or pinkish globs. For reasons unknown some places seem to be better than others for capturing images of these ghostly orbs. Green Hill Cemetery is one of the best.

Ghost photographers should expect a little extra ghostly activity to accompany their art project in Green Hill Cemetery though. Many have reported hearing footsteps follow them along the pathways, particularly in the fall when they can clearly hear unseen feet rustling leaves behind them. The most disturbing ghostly activity in Green Hill though is the smell. Wafts of foul smelling decay often follow people as they walk around the graveyard taking photos and no explainable source for the reek has been found yet.

Captain Video

Usually when one thinks of haunted places they imagine an old cemetery, an abandoned farmhouse, or a former mental institution or orphanage home. Probably one of the last places you'd think is haunted would be a video rental store. Unfortunately it looks like no one has told the ghost at Captain Video, located in Reid Hill Plaza, that she isn't supposed to be there.

No one is sure who the ghostly young woman who is sometimes seen walking around the aisles of Captain Video at night was in life but in death she is, all in all, a pretty boring ghost who receives the attention she does if only for the oddness of where she has decided to spend eternity. She does not seem to be a former employee of the store, no strange deaths or mysterious disappearances there, perhaps in life she was a movie buff and she hates the idea of passing through to the other side until she's seen every movie there is?

Other odd occurrences at Captain Video include strange flashes of colored lights and fuzzy orbs that all appear well after closing time when the store is completely empty.

This Old House

The hundred-and-sixty-year-old house was a ruin when Jeff bought it. It had been first a tavern and then a farm. But times got tough and the farmland surrounding it was sold off bit by bit. When no more land was left to support the owners they abandoned the home. It sat there empty, left to rot and ruin, for years. Jeff was sure that even with as poor of shape as it was in he could restore it with the help of his son.

Their first night in the old house was a bad one. Unused to the noises of a house more than a hundred years old the father and son lay uneasily in their sleeping bags on the scarred hardwood floors for hours before finally being able to drift off to sleep. Worse still, once they did fall asleep, they kept jerking awake sure that someone had just walked into the room with them. Convinced that someone might have broken in Jeff got up at least half a dozen times and walked slowly from room to room armed with a flashlight and a crowbar. He couldn't find anyone. Later on they would find out from an older neighbor who had lived in the house as a young girl that the room they had chosen to sleep in that night was used as a sickroom at some point and that even in her day guests complained that they felt a presence walking in and out of the room all night long.

Jeff soon discovered that the old house was rife with ghostly activity. At night it was normal to see misty glowing shapes float from room to room or hover over their beds. A male spirit seemed to dominate the downstairs while several female ghosts hung around the upstairs. Jeff wondered it they could be the male spirits daughters because they seemed a little afraid of the downstairs presence. The female ghosts would sometimes float around the top of the stairs and the heavy sound of a man's footsteps would soon thunder up towards them, causing the girlish ghosts to flee into different rooms.

The male spirit must have been a smoker in life because, even though no one smoked in the house now, the smell of cigar smoke was common in the formal downstairs living room. Later on one overnight guest, who spent the night on the couch in that room, complained the next morning that he didn't appreci-ate everyone coming downstairs to stare at him sleeping. He refused to believe that all of the living people in the house had spent the night upstairs in their rooms and left in a huff.

The neighbor who had grown up in the house told Jeff to get used to the ghosts, they had been there a long time before he had, and they'd be there long after he was gone. Since, overall, they didn't cause much trouble and were benign presences Jeff didn't mind them so much. The one thing he did care about was the cigar smoke though. He hated the thought of guests smelling it in the house and thinking that he was the one smoking. The neighbor advised him to tell the ghost to take it outside or knock it off. Finally fed up with the smell one day Jeff did just that. No one was more surprised than he was when it worked. Neither the living room, nor any other part of the house for that matter, ever smelled of cigar smoke again.

Widow Susan

The story of widow Susan is one of Amsterdam's most popular legends. She is also one of the city's most widely reported ghosts. Most witnesses report seeing a lady in an old fashioned white dress, walking along Widow Susan Road, sometimes crying but always apparently searching for something. While the ghost has been seen up and down the length of Widow Susan Road, hence the unusual name, most often the spirit seems drawn to the area closest to the river where Saint Michaels Cemetery, Saint Casmir's Cemetery, and Saint Nicholas's Cemetery are all found. Many skeptics pass the story off as nothing more than local legend, stemming from an oddly named road, that just happens to have a grand total of four cemeteries all named after Saints on it, the fourth being Saint John's Cemetery on the other end of the road. However, Widow Susan, whether you believe in the ghost part of the story or not, was once very much a real woman who lived on the road that would come to be named for her all these years later.

Widow Susan was originally named Susan DeGraff and she was a resident of Amsterdam in the early 1800s. Susan was the wife of a farmer and mother to three children. The family led a comfortable life but they were not well of by any means. When her husband Harmanus died Susan faced some hard choices. Somehow she was able to hang onto the house located on one end of what is now Widow Susan Road and raise her three children on her own. She stayed there until her daughter married and then she accompanied the newlyweds to Michigan. Susan DeGraff would remain in Michigan for the rest of her life. When she died her body was returned to Amsterdam where it was buried in Green Hill Cemetery, not very far away from the home where she raised her three children.

It was shortly after the burial that the ghost stories started. Overtime the story has evolved to include quite a few other classic symptoms of haunting, outside of the reports of her ghost visibly walking the street and around the cemeteries. Electronics do not do well at night on Widow Susan Road. Cell phones ring continuously, or refuse to work. CD players stop playing and refuse to turn back on. In one of the more foolish 'ghost hunting' stunts you can imagine Amsterdam teens often dare each other to coast down the hill above the cemeteries with their car headlights turned off while chanting 'Widow Susan' three times. As you turn into the cemetery road many report cars not starting or invisible fingers drawing words or pictures on the frost that forms on the car windows. Whether you believe in the ghost or not it seems an extremely foolhardy way to try and 'prove' ones existence and it's a wonder that more ghosts haven't been created from the car accidents that sometimes happen when drivers miss the unlit cars barreling toward them in the dark.

Like a lot of local legends there are some plot holes in this haunting that make it a little hard to swallow. The ghost of Susan DeGraff is not seen near her home or near the cemetery where she is actually buried. Local lore says the ghost of the widow is distressed because she cannot locate her husband's grave, and thus she is seen most often around the cemeteries located on the road she shares her name with. But the Saint Casmir, Nicholas, and Michael cemeteries did not exist in Susan DeGraff's day, so they could not be the grounds in which her husband was interred. And in life she certainly would have known where her husband had been buried. So why would a ghost haunt cemeteries that have nothing to do with her own burial and cannot possibly be where her husband is buried? Because of these irregularities many would be ghost hunters have given up on the story as nothing more than urban legend. But with a small amount of research a possible explanation has come to light about the intent of the Widow Susan haunting.

Records don't say where Harmanus DeGraff was buried. His grave doesn't appear on any of the (admittedly not well kept) lists of graves dating from his time period. But with a little digging, pun intended, one can find a record from a genealogy buff in the 1920s that lists close to a dozen small, old, and forgotten graveyards in and around Amsterdam. One of the smaller, and already in the 1920s almost totally forgotten, cemeteries was a DeGraff Family Cemetery located just off of Widow Susan Road. This record shows that eight DeGraff graves were still visible and had readable tombstones in the 1920s, and piles of rubble and broken unreadable stones suggested there were quite a few more burials there that names could not be given to. None of these readable graves belonged to a Harmanus DeGraff, even accounting for the sometimes-inconsistent spelling of the time but the graves were all dated between 1823 and 1853. Harmanus died in 1848, putting him right in the correct date range. By the time Susan died more than thirty years later the family cemetery was already well on its way to the ruins that would be discovered in the 1920s and was probably already well forgotten by anyone except a DeGraff family member. This is presumably why Susan DeGraff's body was placed in the newer and better maintained municipal Green Hill Cemetery.

It does not seem to be too far a stretch of the imagination to think that the spirit of Susan DeGraff would have been extremely confused when she found herself interred in Green Hill Cemetery, rather than a plot next to her husband in the family cemetery she must have been expecting. Her distress could only have grown when she discovered her family cemetery, and the grave of her beloved husband, no longer existed. Today it is still possible to find the forgotten remains of the DeGraff family cemetery. Of the eight gravestones that remained nearly intact in the 1920s there are now only two and it seems possible that the cemeteries of Saint Casmir, Saint Nicholas, and Saint Michaels, may cover part of the land that once belonged to the final resting places of generations of DeGraffs. One can't help but imagine that some day as these cemeteries grow a grave digging crew may come across a much older grave in the course of their work, perhaps even the grave Widow Susan has been stymied from finding all of these years, that of her husband Harmanus DeGraff. Perhaps if that discovery is ever made Widow Susan will be at peace and teenagers can stop driving around at night with no headlights endangering everyone they meet.

Clifton Park

T he town of Clifton Park is made up of about a dozen smaller areas known as hamlets. A hamlet is a populated area within another larger recognized town or city that is not itself an incorporated village. Hamlets are unique to New York state in name only. In all other states they are simply known as unincorporated communities or townships. These hamlets are not just neighborhoods located within a town. They, often, have their own labels on maps, have signs welcoming you to their area like any other town, fall inside school districts other than those of the town they are located within, and have their own police stations and other public works.

Ballston Lake, Elnora, Flagler Corners, Grooms Corners, Rexford, and Round Lake are among some of Clifton Park's hamlets. Hauntings and stories set in these hamlets have been included in this Clifton Park chapter.

The Robin's Nest

Originally the Elks had owned, and drastically changed, the old farmhouse. When Robin bought the building in the early 2000s the first goal on her list was the restore it to the way it looked in the homes glory days of the 1840s. Robin realized she was sharing the house with ghosts almost immediately. As soon as the renovation project began tools would turn up missing and, if tools were left out at night, workers would return to find them tucked away in their correct places by morning.

When The Robins Nest opened its doors the ghosts were right there to greet the customers. One older lady took Robin aside and told her that every time she left the room a woman dressed in an old fashioned grey dress would appear and look the place over. The figure disappeared every time Robin walked back into the room. The woman was part of a circle of friends that met periodically at the home of a psychic. She offered to bring the group to Robin's farmhouse to have a meeting. Robin quickly agreed.

When the psychic arrived she fell quickly into a trance and was able to tell Robin that there were many more spirits plaguing the house than just the lady in grey. Upstairs she sensed two small children singing and playing, completely unaware that they were dead. Downstairs there was a constantly revolving group of spirits. Many were former residents of the house but the psychic sensed several of Robin's family members there as well. Robin was skeptical until the psychic passed on messages from these departed love ones that only they could have known.

River Road

George and Vaughan, a musician and folklorist, were very excited when they bought the old 1910 house located on River Road. It needed a little work but they were sure when they were done the house would be restored to its former glory. The first on their list of interior restoration projects were to thoroughly clean and repaint the closets. For some reason every closet in the house smelled of cigar smoke. Vaughan was half inside one of these closets one day shortly after they moved in, repainting the shelves, when she heard a noise behind her. Sure that it was George coming to tell her he was running out for more building supplies she kept on working. After several minutes she began to wonder why he was just standing there not saying anything. A bit irritated she turned around and was surprised to see a very sad looking woman in a blue robe standing behind her watching her paint.

When Vaughan and George bought the house they had joked that it was probably haunted because of its age. Both definitely were firm believers in ghosts and, if they were being honest, were probably actually hoping for a haunted house when they bought the place. But their first few weeks had been so uneventful they gave up on the idea. When Vaughan saw the uninvited guest behind her of course ghost was the first word that popped into her head but the figure was so solid she immediately dismissed the idea. Surprisingly she was not frightened to find a strange woman standing behind her in her own house. In some strange way it looked like the woman belonged there. The lady looked quite frail and, because of the bathrobe and bare feet, Vaughan started to think she was possibly a neighbor's confused elderly parent who had somehow wandered away from home. But before Vaughan could ask the woman who she was and where she lived she heard a voice emanate from the figure.

"Oh, I'm so glad the place is being fixed up" The soft voice told her.

At this point there was no doubt that the house had a ghostly visitor. While the voice came directly from the blue robbed woman her lips never moved and within a few minutes she faded away to nothing. She would never show herself again but as the years went by both George and Vaughan would sometimes sense another being in the room with them even when they were alone.

The mystery of who the woman was answered promptly by a neighbor. He told George one day that the previous owner was a chronically ill woman who had loved the home desperately but was far too sick to keep up maintenance on it.

Hollie

The first clue the new owners of the bed and breakfast had that their inn was haunted was when angry guests started banging on their door in the middle of the night. The couple said they had just gotten into bed in their guestroom when the door to the room opened. An older woman in an out of date nightgown entered the room holding the hand of a small child. The two smiled and chatted happily as they walked around the room. After making a quick pass around the room the woman came over to the bed and kindly tucked the guests in. As the spirits left they turned the lights out behind them. Needless to say the guests were not comforted and left to go to an un-haunted hotel for the night.

It was not until they started mentioning the strange tale to neighbors that anyone told them that they had been seeing the ghost of the older woman for years. She was often seen hovering around the outside of the house and looking from the windows at the passersby. While the house had been sitting empty neighbors would sometimes see lights turn on and off, even though they knew the electricity had been cut, and music poured out from the house onto the night air. This ghost was enough of a fixture in the neighborhood that it even had a name, Hollie.

Originally known as Elmcrest House the building had been a private family home for several generations. Hollie had inherited the home in the early 1900s from her own father and lived out a quiet and uneventful life. When her own son and daughter in law inherited the house they were amazed at the ghostly activity, something Hollie had never mentioned in all her years in residence. Doors slammed open and shut of their own accord and the sound of music would draw the listener into rooms where they could see the ghostly image of a party superimposed over that of the modern day rooms. Shortly after moving in a white cat appeared that no one had ever seen before. The cat stalked something unseen around the outside of the house and tried frantically to get inside. Some witnesses said later on that the cat didn't meow properly but seemed to say the name 'Helen'. Helen had been Hollie's most loyal housekeeper. After being denied entry into the house the cat walked off on its own and was not seen again.

The Country Club on Riverview Road

The country club got an unusual start. After all it's not many that begin as dairy farms! Many years before the country club opened it was the Zoller Farm, owned by two brothers Frank and Jessie. The Zollers sold their products under the name Walhalla Dairy. Frank Zoller would go on to earn international regard for his ability to breed prize winning Brown Swiss Cattle, a breed almost unknown in the United States because the Federal government prohibited the importation of this breed shortly after the Zoller's received their first herd. Sadly in 1932 Frank Zoller would be gored by one of his own prizewinning bulls and died. The farm managed to struggle on without him but it closed its operations down less than thirty years after his death.

The country club kept many of the original farm buildings and they are still used today. The farmhouse once shared by the Zoller brothers is, today, the clubhouse. There is at least one other old timer lingering around the greens. Maintenance crews and early morning golfers have seen the spirit of Frank Zoller quite often in the early hours of the dawn, trudging sleepily from the clubhouse off across the lawn to do his morning chores in buildings that no longer exist. By the time the sun starts to climb a little higher in the sky Franks spirit burns off like an early morning fog, but he is always out bright and early the next morning to start his work all over again.

Cohoes

The Van Schaick Family Cemetery

The Van Schaik Family Cemetery is one of the creepier haunts out there, even as far as ghosts go. The most commonly reported ghostly phenomenon is the sound of ghostly voices calling through the graveyard gates, urging people to come in. Many people, assuming it is teenagers pulling a prank, have walked through the gates to confront the kids and tell them to go home. Once inside the cemetery they never find anyone living.

The cemetery is full of both male and female spirits, dressed in a variety of fashions from several different time periods. They seem to be unaware of the living people who pass through their final resting spot so it is unlikely they are the ones trying to lure passersby inside. Visitors have seen ghosts, all seemingly from different decades, group together to chat and walk, and sometimes even see female spirits leading the ghosts of small children by the hand as they walk endlessly around the Van Schaik Family Cemetery.

The Cohoes Music Hall

This more than one hundred and thirty year old music hall is the fourth oldest surviving one in the country. It was the brainchild of two Cohoes businessmen, James Martsen and William Acheson. They built the entire structure for $60,000, a rather large sum for its day. The Music Hall was originally famous as a vaudeville stage. In its heyday its stage was graced by such legendary presences as Buffalo Bill Cody, Jimmy Durante, and Sarah Bernhardt. In time, like many of the countries great theaters and halls, the building fell into ruin and was in danger of being demolished. At the last possible moment the Cohoes Music Hall was added to the National Register of Historic Places and reopened, bringing theater and educational programs to the city of Cohoes to this day.

Eva Tanguay was one of the Vaudeville stars that lit up the stage in the early days of the Cohoes Music Hall. Eva was born in Canada but even as a young child showed such an interest in the performing arts that her family moved her to the United States. When she was twelve they arrived in Cohoes.

Eva was a pretty girl, though not an extraordinary beauty. What she lacked in talent she made up for in enthusiasm and scandal. Eva would sometimes spend twice her salary taking ads out in local papers to promote herself and when she couldn't afford to buy news coverage she created it. Eva faked her own kidnapping and filed false reports of stolen jewelry to keep the media attention on what she was doing next.

It has long been said in advertising that sex sells, and the lesson was not lost on Eva Tanguay. She sometimes appeared on stage wearing flimsy costumes made up of just dollar bills and pennies. Her trademark was raunchy suggestive songs that seem pretty innocent today, though they caused an uproar in her time. Some of her more famous songs were "Go As Far As You Like", "It's All Been Done Before But Not the Way I Do It", and "I Want Someone to go Wild With Me". At the height of her career she was the highest paid entertainer in the country, pulling in $3500 a week in 1910.

Eva's extravagant lifestyle couldn't last forever and she lost millions in the stock market crash of 1929. Even so a year later she retired from the stage forever. She would die in relative obscurity and extreme poverty in California in 1947. Among her personal papers was a half finished autobiography she entitled "Up and Down the Ladder". The popular Hearst newspapers published three excerpts from the unfinished book after her death. Fans couldn't help but think that wherever she was she was enjoying having the papers printing her name again.

Eva is gone but is definitely not forgotten. That goes doubly so at the Cohoes Music Hall where her ghost is said to still haunt the stage. Her lavishly dressed spirit has been seen waiting patiently in the wings, as if waiting for her cue to come on stage. More than one performer has been surprised to find their props missing and an old fashioned one put in its place. A few of these items have been directly linked to being identical to something Eva herself used on stage.

She is not the Cohoes Music Halls only spirit. Stagehands working late into the night have heard, on many occasions, the sounds of a couple arguing when the theater was otherwise empty. The female half of this couple is not thought to be Eva Tanguay. Eva, in sharp contrast to her onstage persona, preferred no drama when it came to romance and her relationship with her manager was near legendary for its lack of conflict. Few men, it seemed, were willing to test the limits of the woman who became famous as the "I Don't Care Girl", another of her runaway hits.

It is possible that the ghost heard arguing with her lover is that of the ghost that is known only as the Black Lady. The Black Lady has appeared many times over the years standing in the second row of the upper balcony. She is described as wearing a 1940s style black dress. The Black Lady is described by many as an angry spirit with a mean look in her eye.

Starting in the year 2000, on the opening night of 'Grease' the elevator began to malfunction. The doors open and shut erratically and the elevator car traveled between floors even when no one had pushed the call button. Handymen looked the elevator over carefully for the malfunction but were never able to explain what was wrong. The strange problem lasted solely for the length of the run of the play. It has not been duplicated since and no cause was ever found.

Cohoes Falls

The haunting at Cohoes Falls is an interesting one because there are two different stories about whom the ghost is and how that ghost ended up there, even though there really is only one ghost here. The shorter and simpler of the two legends tells us simply that a young Native American girl was paddling her canoe up the river one day when she misjudged the current and plunged over the falls, meeting her demise on the rocks below. On nights with a full moon she is said to be visible frantically paddling away from the falls as though trying to save her life.

The second story is somewhat similar but a little more involved. In this version of the story a young Seneca man named Occuna falls in love with a white settler who built her cabin near what is present day Cohoes. Despite it being a scandal in their time Occuna and his maiden fell madly in love and enjoyed an extended period of courting. They could often be seen floating along the river gazing, love struck, into each other's eyes. One evening they gazed at each other a little too long and abruptly found themselves in the pull created by the falls. The couple tried valiantly to paddle away and save themselves but there was no escaping the current.

The canoe tumbled over the falls. Occuna, the Seneca warrior, was lost immediately. But his young maiden was thrown clear of the rocks and was able to swim to shore. She lived an uneventful life but when she died, many years later, the sightings began of a young Native American man paddling frantically away from the top of the falls.

So the question remains: which version of the legend, and which ghost, is the one that is still sometimes seen atop the Cohoes Falls? It seems most likely that the spirit seen is Occuna who, because of his long uncut hair witnesses mistake for a young girl, rather than a young man.

'Tis the Season

A haunted cemetery, a haunted Music Hall, a haunted waterfall. What more could Cohoes have to offer? How about a haunted pizza parlor? Former owners of this long-standing Cohoes eatery swear they had a ghostly gourmet in their kitchen. They would leave work at night with everything clean and set up for the next day. But that didn't mean that was how the kitchen would appear when they came to open the next morning. The ghost that plagued their kitchen seemed to have very definite ideas of where it thought the utensils and cooking supplies belonged and would continuously rearrange the kitchen to these incomprehensible placements. Luckily it never affected the taste of the pizza.

Above the pizza shop are two apartments and the tenants had as many run ins with ghosts as the restaurant employees had. A tenant on the second floor complained that the spirit of a man in an old-fashioned pin striped suit continually occupied her rocking chair. The other neighbors had a dog that seemed to be tormented by something they could not see. The dog would bark at thin air and then run away from the same spot with its tail tucked between its legs as if it had just been threatened. Oftentimes the dog would simply refuse to enter certain rooms at all.

The haunting throughout the building seemed to get worse when the holiday season rolled around. One night just before Christmas a family living upstairs were awoken to the sound of a raucous party in their own living room, complete with loud music. As soon as they walked into the room and flicked on the lights all of the noises stopped abruptly and the only thing out of place was the Christmas tree that had somehow been moved to the other side of the room, every ornament in place and intact.

Glens Falls

Anna

The Chapman Historical Museum, located at 348 Glen Street, in a former residence known as the DeLong House, is a carefully restored 19th century home that highlights what life was like in the area in the 1800s. Considering that a least one of the 1800s residents has stayed on in the building one has to think that the Glens Falls/Queensbury Historical Association maybe did too good of a job in restoring and preserving the building.

From outside the Chapman Historical Museum, even on Mondays when the museum is closed, passersby sometimes see the window curtains part and a young woman peer out at them. She has long brown hair, parted in the middle, and wears a simple pink dress, cut in an old fashioned style. This is Anna. In life she was a housekeeper for Zopher DeLong, the wealthy Glens Falls merchant who built the home on Glen Street in 1868.

More rarely Anna has also been seen by people inside the building as well. Some visitors have mistaken her for an employee in period costume. Others have said she disappears into thin air when confronted by the living. It is unclear why Anna, only an employee at the home, has stayed on after death while Zopher and his son John seem to have passed on so easily.

Blimps

On August 19, 1974 there was a wave of U.F.O sightings in and around Glens Falls. Most of those calling in to local news media and police reported seeing multiple blimp-like objects that seemed to be covered in flashing colored lights. These strange blimps would hover in place before dashing away at impossible speeds.

By midnight more than a hundred people gathered along Dix Avenue in Glens Falls to watch the aeronautics of these strange crafts. Radio stations sent reporters and the police arrived for crowd control. When local police confirmed seeing the unusual craft state police were sent over from Saratoga. One cruiser saw a craft similar to ones they had been receiving reports about fly low over Saratoga Lake, draw water from it, and then zip away.

By one o'clock that morning police estimated there were close to five hundred people lining Dix Avenue, drawn by the increasingly strange radio reports. Several people who lived along the street said the next day that they awoke in their beds, unable to move, seeing the strange aircraft floating outside their windows and shining colored lights over them.

Albany Civil Air Patrol sent their own units to investigate. They clocked the large objects moving at unheard of speeds and were unable to identify them as any known human aircraft. One by one the oversized blimps flew away, never to be seen in Glens Falls or the surrounding area again. The police did their best to disperse the crowds along Dix Avenue as quickly as they could but people refused to leave, hoping the ships would come back.

St. Mary's Church

At least one of the priests at St. Mary's is so dedicated that he has continued on with his work even after death. Those walking by the church on Warren Street around midnight are sometimes surprised to see the windows aglow and the sound of music and singing emanating from the very locked, and very empty, building. From the sounds of things one would think there was a full congregation inside in the midst of worship.

Those who have had reason to be inside the church late at night have had a very different ghostly experience. Many have reported seeing the spirit of a priest going through the motions of giving mass in the deserted building, acting as though the pews were filled with parishioners.

St. Mary's Church was founded in 1848 and since then the Glens Falls area has been serviced by any number of priests. So far no one has been able to identify the one who remains so dedicated to bringing the peace of the lord to his flock.

Latham

Guptills Woods

The patch of woods on Pollack Road known as Guptills Woods don't seem to be haunted. But the old house located within them certainly is. Many people walking through the woods are drawn to the home by the sound of unearthly singing. Those who have gone inside to explore the home have come across floating cold spots, strange colored flashing orbs and, most chillingly, glowing eyes in the darkness. The eyes have never been seen as part of a face, they are said to be disembodied eyes that float up out of the darkness, as if daring the explorer to go any further.

To War

Behind the Woodlands Apartment building on Kenwood Court there is a fairly well preserved cemetery dating from the Revolutionary War. The graveyard is small, comprised of a mere dozen or so tombstones but the old soldiers certainly are a lively bunch!

The voices of men raised in good cheer are often heard coming from the cemetery. On full moon nights they say that the sound of beating drums drowns out the voices.

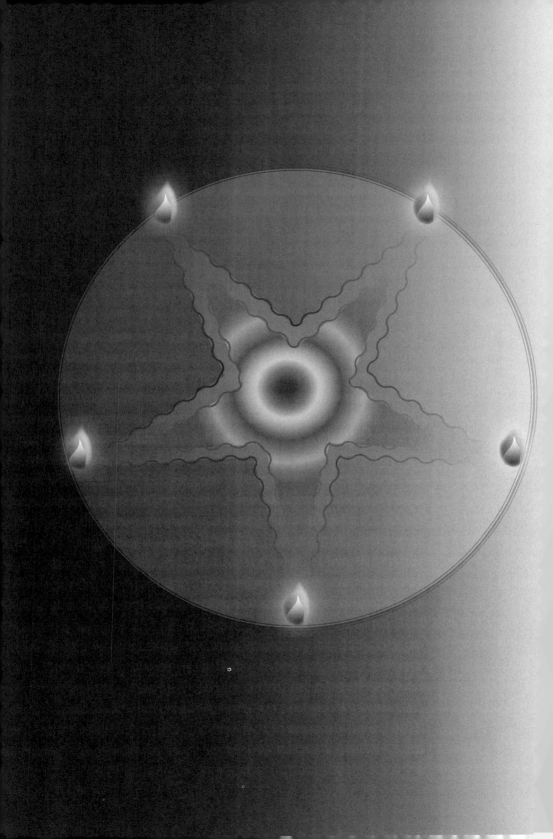

Menands

Albany Rural Cemetery

The way we look at death and cemeteries has changed a lot over the years. Originally the norm when a family member died was that the deceased's family took care of the body themselves and buried it on their own property in a family plot. As time went on and the Capital District developed more it proved impractical, and something of a health hazard, to have families stashing bodies here and there on their own properties. Churches soon took over the duty of interring bodies after death. But the churches had no more access to unlimited land than their parishioners did. By 1801 the cities had taken over the care and maintenance of burial grounds. A municipal graveyard opened in Albany that same year in what is now the eastern side of Washington Park. The graveyard was split into sections and each slice was for the use of a different area church.

The idea was so popular that the churches actually began removing bodies already long buried on the grounds of their own cemeteries and moved them into this municipal burying ground. But funerary practices in the 1800s and earlier were not what they are today. It was rare for bodies to be embalmed and, if coffins were even used, they were made from the thinnest cheapest pine boards that could be purchased. Churches dug up bodies to find them long decomposed and their coffins gone, if they had ever existed in the first place. To make matters worse many tombstones were cracked, or unreadable after the passage of time, or had just never been there to begin with. Needless to say the moving of bodies caused a great deal of confusion in all of the effected burial grounds. While undoubtedly the churches made every effort to move each body, intact, and place the correct tombstone with it mistakes were made.

This process went on until 1841. Church cemeteries were a mess and the new municipal cemetery was just as confused. To make matters even worse the municipal cemetery began to flood every spring, which held up the burial of fresh bodies and only added to the confusion when moving the old. Fed up the public began to demand that something be done.

The city decided to create an all-new 'rural' cemetery, located well outside of the city limits. This would cut down on the health hazard to residents with the constant movement and burial of bodies. Plus I'm sure it occurred to the city fathers that much of the outcry would quiet down when their constituents no longer had to look at the flooded confused mess of the municipal cemetery every day. As they say, out of sight and out of mind, making a rural cemetery outside of the city limits would serve a double duty. The plan worked. Within a few short years the Albany Rural Cemetery was dedicated and the first burials were begun. In time every body within the municipal cemetery would be moved to this rural cemetery outside of town though the strictest of rules were created to make sure that, as much as possible, this was done in a methodical and orderly fashion. The modern beautifully maintained cemetery was such a success that it continues to be used today, though it is now part of Menands rather than the city of Albany itself.

The records at Albany Rural Cemetery is something of a Capital District Who's Who list. You'll find former Albany mayors, Revolutionary War Generals, and even the Twenty-fourth President of the United States, Chester Arthur, buried here. Even so the most famous residents are the ghosts.

Albany Rural Cemetery sometimes looks like something out of a scary movie. Ghostly black cars arrive in large groups and black dressed figures amass around them. But these are not a collection of cars from a funeral home there for a burial. The cars and people are as insubstantial as mist. When the police have been called they find no one near the area and no evidence that any have been in the cemetery. Few witnesses have had the courage to try and confront the darkly dressed masses but those that have report the figures slowly fade from view when approached.

The cemetery's most frequently seen spirits are not as worrisome though. The ghostly figures of a young couple, holding hands and clad in, of all things, pajamas are seen more often than the dark suited figures. They tour the grounds, passing through tombstones and oblivious to the living, before fading away into thin air.

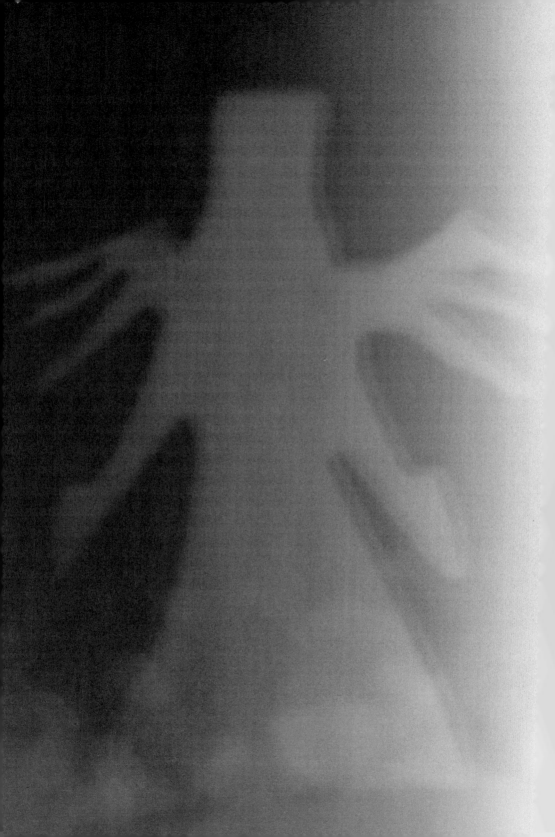

Rensselaer

The Guardian Angel

Doreen never thought she lived in a haunted house. She didn't even think she believed in ghosts. But a few years ago all of that changed in just a single night. The young mother was awoken in the early hours of the morning when she felt her husband getting into bed. Just as she was about to fall back to sleep she felt him start to bounce up and down on the mattress.

"Are you kidding?" She yelled. "It's three in the morning!"

But when she turned to confront him the room was empty except for her! At that very instant she heard the sound, clear on the other side of the house, of her husband opening up the refrigerator looking for a late night snack. Doreen was not immediately unnerved, more than anything she feared an intruder might be in the house. She dashed into the living room to tell her husband what had happened and together they decided they better begin checking each room, making sure they were empty and all the windows firmly shut and locked.

The first place they went to was their infant daughter's bedroom. Approaching the door they heard the little girl choking and coughing. Rushing in they found the baby's windpipe was almost entirely blocked. Quickly they cleared it so the child could breathe. But there was no doubt that something far more tragic would have occurred if Doreen hadn't been awakened in the middle of the night.

It wasn't until the unseen visitor interceded in a few more mishaps, all relatively minor when compared to a choking baby, that Doreen started to joke around about their guardian angel. She's still not entirely sure she believes in ghosts but she believes some kind of presence is watching over her family.

Saratoga Springs

Saratoga Springs has always been a popular tourist destination. It is a town of a little under 30,000 people but the population swells to many times that each summer with the opening season of the famous Saratoga Raceway. Saratoga Springs has a reputation for being the cultural center of the Capital District, as it is the summer home of both the New York City ballet and the Philadelphia orchestra. There are currently more golf courses in Saratoga Springs than museums and the community hopes to become as much as a national hotspot for golf tourists as it is for horse racing fans.

The Saratoga Race Course is the oldest continuously operating thoroughbred track in the country. It was been a popular tourist destination since the late 1800s.

Yaddo: House of Shadows

The land that Yaddo, an artists community just minutes up the street from Saratoga's famous racetrack, sits on has been the site of several farms, a mill, a tavern where Edgar Allan Poe is thought to have written part of his famous poem "The Raven", and the scene of several family tragedies. It has been called Yaddo since 1881, when Spencer and Katrina Trask purchased it. Yaddo is a mispronunciation of 'shadow', a word that the Trask's four-year-old daughter Christina thought was fitting for their new home but had trouble saying it correctly.

It is, perhaps, no surprise that the little girl would associate her new home with gloom. The Trasks moved to Saratoga Springs from New York City after the death of their five year old child, Alanson. There was hope that the move would be a new beginning for the family but their incredible bad luck seemed to have followed them upstate. A few years after moving to the 400 acre plot Katrina Trask contracted diphtheria, a respiratory disease that killed tens of thousands of people in the United States every year until a vaccine was created in the 1920s. Katrina Trask would survive her diphtheria, though the disease would disable her for life. All of the Trask children caught the disease from their mother and all died within one week of each other. The next year Katrina would give birth to a dead baby.

This entrance to Yaddo hides a stunning fifty five room mansion that has been a temporary home to artists like John Cheever, Langston Hughes, and Truman Capote. Edgar Allen Poe wrote part of 'The Raven' in a tavern that once stood where the home stands now.

The Trask family troubles were not soon over. In 1891 a fire decimated their Saratoga Springs home. The Yaddo Mansion that exists today is the house that was built to replace the one lost to this fire. But this immense fifty-five room gothic-Victorian mansion undoubtedly brought little solace to the now childless Trasks. Spencer Trask would lose an eye in an automobile accident in Boston and would later die on New Years Eve 1909 in a freak train accident.

Katrina Trask fared no better than her husband. In 1913 she was victim to several heart attacks that further limited her ability to move around the grounds of Yaddo. Despite her ill health she was courted and married by her husband's friend and business partner George Foster Peabody. She died less than a year later.

Today the Yaddo Mansion is strictly off limits to anyone but resident artists, though the public is welcome to enjoy the rose gardens outside.

Despite their personal hardships the Trasks were fabulously wealthy even by today's standards. Spencer Trask was a prominent Wall Street banker and financed several entrepreneurs, Thomas Edison among them. Both Katrina and Spencer Trask were serious patrons of the arts. The Trasks were prominent members of the National Arts Club and in life their homes both in Brooklyn and Saratoga Springs were havens where artists of all mediums could enjoy a fine meal and even finer conversation. It is no surprise, given their love of the arts and the early deaths of all their immediate heirs, that the Trask estate would go towards creating an artist's community that would live on long after their deaths.

The first artists moved into Yaddo in 1926. Since that time the Yaddo Mansion has been a temporary home to more than six thousand artists. Truman Capote, John Cheever, Kenneth Fearing, Langston Hughes, and Robert Lowell have all called Yaddo home at one point or another. Sylvia Plath would stay there for a year as a guest of her husband Ted Hughes, who was invited to be an artist in residence. All together Yaddo artists have been awarded 63 Pulitzer Prizes, 25 MacArthur Fellowships, 58 National Book Awards, and 1 Nobel Prize, with these numbers always growing.

The house and the artist's retreats at Yaddo are strictly off limits to visitors. The point of the retreat is to give artists space and privacy to work on their art. Visitors are allowed to visit the formal gardens that the Trasks modeled after the ones they saw at European castles and the yard is dotted with beautiful statues and fountains. The fountains have given rise to a particularly tenacious myth that the Trasks abandoned the property because one of their small children drowned in a fountain while trying to catch one of the ornamental fish they were stocked with in the Trasks day. You will even find visitors who swear they've seen the spirit of a drowned child walking from the house to fountain or back again, and can cause some embarrassment when you point out that none of the admittedly unlucky Trask children drowned at Yaddo.

The rose garden, and its statues, were modeled after those surrounding European castles.

That is not to say that ghosts and odd occurrences don't happen at Yaddo. Given the terrible tragedies of the Trask family and the sometimes eccentric or sensitive people that would come to live there after the Trasks passed on it's a wonder that guests don't have to elbow ghosts out of their way to get a good look at heirloom roses or Italian statuary. The spirit most often seen inside and outside the house is that of a woman in a long flowing dress. People debate whether this ghost is Katrina Trask herself, finding comfort in the good that has risen up from the incredible hardship of her life, or that of Elizabeth Ames, Yaddo's first director. Several witnesses have said the dress the ghost wears exactly matches one worn by Katrina Trask in a portrait that is said to still hang in the mansion today. Others swear the spirit is a dead ringer for Elizabeth Ames who manned the helm at Yaddo for more than half a century. Of course, there is nothing to say that Yaddo can't have two lady ghosts walking its hallways and enjoying the garden.

The rose garden is the scene of electrical disturbances thought to be caused by the ghost of Katrina Trask or Elizabeth Ames.

One of the second floor bedrooms in Yaddo has a spirit all its own. This ghost is all work and no play. Artists who have spent time in this room complain that whenever they cut loose and take a break from their artistic endeavors the ghost starts to open and shut the windows loudly. It will not stop until they go back to work.

The house is not the only place in Yaddo that is haunted. Orb photographs are common in the rose garden and in one southwest corner cameras malfunction entirely. A few people have had cell phone problems while walking the garden pathways, particularly when standing near the statues. Cell phones that previously worked just fine ring ceaselessly and the caller ID shows weird number combinations that could never be a working phone number.

The Witch of Saratoga

The Witch of Saratoga was, for many years, almost as much of a landmark as the town's racetrack. She lived in a shack deep in a forested ravine in the shadow of Mount Vista, just a few miles north of the village of Saratoga Springs. She was known for her wild tangle of hair and flashing angry black eyes. In the early 1800s those few brave souls from town that wanted a potion to help a sick family member or a glimpse into their future would make the long trek through the woods to the witch's shack. In the summer months the witch would make the hike herself and come into town to tell the fortunes of the tourists who came to bath in the city's hot springs. Though you would have had a hard time getting anyone in town to admit that they had partaken of the Witches services she managed to eek out a meager but passable existence this way for almost all her life. Besides her title of Witch, many referred to her as the Mistress of the Whirlwinds, as her love of storms was well known. Many a traveler would arrive in the village with stories that they had seen an old woman climbing from crag to crag, in the most daunting of weather, to stand atop Mount Vista bearing the full force of the storm.

No one who knew the old wretch could have ever imagined her origins or how she came to be the Witch of Saratoga. Her name was Angeline Tubbs and as a young woman her beauty was renowned throughout the area. Many suitors tried for her hand but she turned them all down flat. Angeline, it seemed, was hoping to make a profitable match. But like many sixteen-year-old ladies, both then and now, her good intentions were led astray by a sweet-talking stranger and a lot of promises that came to nothing. During the Revolutionary War Angeline, quite openly, became the mistress of General John Burgoyne, leader of the British forces. Burgoyne would go on to be defeated at the famous Battle of Saratoga, an important turning point in the war, and was forced to retreat. Burgoyne had promised all along to marry Angeline as soon as the war was decided but when he fell from grace after his defeat at Saratoga he paused in his retreat only long enough to try and kill the young girl who had been sharing his officer's tent for so many months.

Angeline survived the attack from her lover but never seemed to get over her heartbreak. She fled to the woods surrounding Saratoga Springs and began work on the shack she would live in all her life. She never took a husband and would always live alone except for a stunning multitude of cats. Angeline lived that way until 1865, dying of old age at a staggering 101 years of age.

To this day travelers sometimes report seeing a strange figure on top of Mount Vista, though today few people know the name of this bare outcropping of rock or who the figure is. The most famous sighting was in the 1930s when a Yaddo resident artist was driving up Route 9 and stopped to pick some interesting wild flowers he saw growing along the road. Following the flowers deeper and deeper into the woods away from the roadside the artist was caught unawares by a passing thundershower. He took refuge under a large pine and decided to wait it out before attempting to make his way back to the car. He was drawn from his hiding space though when he heard the sounds of footsteps and a woman singing to herself happily as though she was oblivious to the rain. He looked around everywhere trying to find the source of the noises, so clear above the sounds of the storm, but was stunned when he looked above him and saw an old woman standing atop the cliff, with her arms outstretched to the flashing lightning, and her wild hair whipping in the strong winds. By the time the lightning flashed a second time the figure was gone even though the artist hadn't seen her climb down.

The Adelphi Hotel

In life John Morrissey was one of those larger than life figures. He gained fame first as a bare-knuckle boxer, would go on to become both a State Senator and a U.S Congressman, and at one point was a notorious gang member who acted as a collection agent, a euphemism for thug, for the Irish mob. As a young man, desperate to escape the poverty he was mired in while living in Troy, he traveled to California to pan for gold. Morrissey's gold mine never panned out but the man did develop a taste for gambling, something he appeared to have a real talent for. Eventually Morrissey returned to the Capital District and was instrumental in creating the Saratoga Race Course and started a casino in town that attracted the rich and famous of his day. Eventually he would own a share of at least sixteen casinos. One year after the opening of the Adelphi Hotel Morrissey would move in as a permanent lodger. Soon after Morrissey passed away in his Adelphi Hotel room, a victim of either pneumonia or a stroke.

Though modestly sized by the standards of the Saratoga Springs hotels of its day the Adelphi has always had a reputation for luxury and impeccable service.

In death Morrissey is just as colorful and just as lively. Many guests who stay in the room where he passed on feel his presence. Some still even lose money to him! Guests who leave a few coins lying around usually come to find them missing later on, even if they were in the room the entire time and no intruder could have entered.

The Adelphi was and is an important Saratoga landmark. At the time it was built it was considered one of the city's smaller hotels. The goal of the Adelphi was to cater to a discriminating clientele and offer personal service that they felt their oversized hotel neighbors could not. Now, over a hundred years later, most of Saratoga's giant hotels are gone. The two largest hotels in the city have been demolished and now a Borders Bookstore stands in part of their lots. The Adelphi's doors are still open for business.

The wedding cake inspired Victorian-Gothic structure has at least one other ghost. She is described as a beautiful woman in a blue dress who walks the hallways and guestrooms shutting off lights and closing doors. No one is sure who the frugal spirit may be.

The Adelphi is a Saratoga landmark, with its gingerbread trim and its colorful ghosts.

The Washington Bath House

While today Saratoga Springs is probably most famous for the Saratoga Race Course, the country's oldest continuously operating thoroughbred track and some say the oldest organized sports venue in the United States period, in the early days of Saratoga Springs history people flocked to the town for healing not gambling and racing. The landscape is dotted with natural mineral springs that were thought to have healing properties for a variety of ailments. The same geological fault that has resulted in the Adirondack Mountains is also the source of the dozens of mineral springs in the area. Deep cracks within the Earth allow carbonated mineral water to seep up to the planets surface from thousands of feet below.

In fact, it is because of the mineral springs that the city exists at all today. Native Americans, who believed in the healing powers of the waters here, brought an injured British soldier, Sir William Johnson, to the area to have his war wounds treated by the waters. Sir William Johnson talked up his stay enough that within nine years permanent settlers had begun to arrive in droves. The tourist trade has always been Saratoga Springs strong point. In a very short amount of time it would become as famous for its enormous opulent hotels as it was for horse racing and mineral springs.

People traveled to Saratoga Springs from all over the world to drink the mineral water and bath in it. At one point as many as seven million bottles of Saratoga Springs water a year were being sold around the world. Within thirty years the water tables around the city were noticeably lower. The state of New York passed laws to try and curb the water industry, in order to preserve the natural mineral springs, but the merchants who had grown wealthy from the industry fought the laws. In 1912, in a last ditch effort to save this vital piece of New York's history, the state set aside eight hundred acres of land as a state park and took over ownership of the springs. In time this Saratoga Springs State Park would grow to a staggering twenty-two hundred acres.

That is not to say that the state's motives were entirely altruistic. A few years after setting aside the land for conservation the state began construction of its own 'medical' bath houses. During the 1930s and 1940s around 200,000 medical baths were given in the four bathhouses the state of New York had built.

The Washington Bath House was the first of the four. It opened in 1920 and featured both private and semi-private rooms. It was quickly followed by the Lincoln Baths and two Roosevelt Bath Houses, one for men and one for women. At the time the Roosevelt facilities were the most modernly equipped bathhouses to be found in the entire world, and they featured a level of privacy that was near unheard of, even when compared to the bathhouses run by the areas most luxurious hotels. Today the Roosevelt Baths are waiting for a team of restoration experts to come and bring them back to the beauty they were known for in their heyday, since they declined rapidly after being converted in a Veterans hospital and then a health club. The Lincoln Baths now house State Police offices.

The Washington Bath House is now home to the only museum in the country that focuses on American dance. Since 1986 it has been the National Museum of Dance and Hall of Fame. Visitors come to the museum to see costumes worn by famous dancers, videos of performances, and some even come to learn how to dance themselves. But there is at least one room that is not open to the public. Formerly used as one of the famous baths this room is now stacked to the rafters with early 20th Century health equipment- though the untrained eye might have trouble telling so! Those who have seen the room say it looks more like a torture chamber than a place filled with items used in medical care.

The National Museum of Dance is well aware of the treasure trove this room contains and has been trying to find a way to open the room as a museum of its own, while not taking away from its expressed purpose of recognizing and showcasing achievements in dance. There has been at least one loud dissenter to the idea. Since the project has been considered a ghostly presence has made itself known in the room. No one is sure who the ghost is or why they seem to be so opposed to the project. The spirit has never been seen but has certainly been felt in the form of a roaming cold spot that seems to be entirely confined to this one small room. Any visitors to the room who have mentioned the proposed project in front of the ghost have been surprised to see small objects begin to levitate and attachments on the larger pieces of equipment move around as if by their own volition.

The Old Bryan Inn

Given Saratoga's immediate popularity as a tourist spot it is not surprising that one of the first buildings to be constructed in the town was an inn. It began as a humble cabin, overlooking High Rock Spring, which was built by Dirck Schoughten. But Dirck quickly came to heads with the local Native American population who used the High Rock Spring as a source of healing. He left the area within just a few months of his arrival. Within a years time the Arnold family had taken over the cabin, threw numerous additions onto the crude structure and began operating an inn. After that the inn passed quickly through the hands of several different owners, most staying a year or less.

In 1787 a Revolutionary War hero, Alexander Bryan, bought the inn. It would remain in his family until the 1900s and the building near High Rock Spring retains the family name to this day. Some of the ghosts at the Old Bryan Inn seem to date from Alexander Bryan's day as well. There are at least two men in

Revolutionary War uniforms who are seen from time to time milling around the modern incarnation of the Old Bryan Inn. During one renovation project the spirits seemed to be seen more often than usual. Oftentimes in the bar area glasses are seen levitating. Most people think it's the soldier ghosts, perhaps enjoying a toast. These spirits have also been seen walking around blowing out candles at the end of the evening.

They are not the most famous ghosts at this Saratoga Springs restaurant. That title is firmly in the hands of a ghost known as Eleanor. She has been credited with events as varied as massaging an overtaxed manager's neck, shuffling papers around the front desk, and swinging chandeliers at will. One time a two hundred pound palm tree was found moved clear across the room and the only explanation anyone could come up with was that Eleanor didn't like where it was placed originally.

Former residents of the inn dispute the ghosts name but not her presence. In the 1950s two young children there were at the center of several ghostly incidents. Several times they saw a woman in a green Victorian style dress. Sometimes the ghost even called them by name. This spirit would go around the house turning on faucets and opening and shutting the door to the attic. When the family moved they found a green dress that was identical to the one they had seen the ghost wearing. Originally it had belonged to an ancestor of theirs named Beatrice. They are convinced to this day that the ghost known commonly as Eleanor is actually their ancestor Beatrice. The confusion over the names only grows when taking into account that at least one bar patron has said the ghost communicated with them and declared her name to be Ida.

The Union Gables Bed and Breakfast

Like many of Saratoga Spring's historic inns the Union Gables Bed and Breakfast has had an interesting, and ghostly, history. This Queen Anne style mansion was built in 1901 for George Crippen, a dry goods merchant. In 1920 the founder of The Glens Falls Times, Charles Furness, bought it. The Furness family didn't hold on to the house on Union Street for much longer than Mr. Crippen. They sold it to Skidmore College, who used the building as a freshman girl's dorm for thirty-four years. It was not until the late 1970's that Skidmore revamped their campus and built new dormitories; selling the old dormitory building that still had the Furness family name on a plaque outside. At this point the building fell into use as a group home. It did not become an inn until after a major renovation project was completed in 1992.

The ghost stories surrounding Union Gables have been told since the time it was a girl's dorm, at the very least. But, because it is rare to find students on a college campus who don't claim their dormitories are haunted, the stories were never looked at as being very credible. If the Furness family or Crippens had any run ins with ghosts they certainly weren't sharing the news. But by the time the time Union Gables opened its doors as an inn the ghosts were a little hard to ignore.

Each room in the Union Gables has a personality, and decorating scheme, of its own. In order to keep prospective guests from having to tromp up and down the stairs to find the right room for their needs the Union Gables owner set up a computer in the lobby, complete with a virtual tour program. Just before opening day the owner decided to take the virtual tour herself to check for any glitches. It was a good thing she checked. On the virtual tour, where one of the guest rooms should be, she was surprised to see a smoke filled room complete with card table and a few whiskey sipping gentleman. The owner blinked a few times and the image was gone. The virtual tour now showed the room just as it should be.

The Union Gables Bed and breakfast is haunted by college co-eds!

But events soon proved that the vision was more than an unusual computer glitch. Shortly after taking the virtual tour a maid came running down the stairs. They were about to open and one of the guest room doors that had never stuck before was so tightly shut she worried the lock was somehow jammed into place. The keys turned easily but still the door refused to open. Going upstairs the Innkeeper was surprised to find that the stuck door was the one that led to the very room that she had seen as a men's game room on the computer. Together the owner and maid were able to wrestle the door open. The room appeared just as it should be but it reeked of cigar smoke and men's aftershave. In time other employees would speak out about the odd occurrences they had in this room. Several had actually seen the card table and four men sitting around it. Others would get the sudden scent of cigar smoke in the air, even though smoking was not allowed in the inn.

Card playing gentlemen are not the only ghosts in the Union Gables Bed and Breakfast. A few months after those spirits made themselves known employees were startled to hear the sound of running footsteps, slamming doors, and raucous giggling throughout the empty inn. Upstairs they saw the images of young women in outdated clothes and a room they had never seen before superimposed over the guest rooms they were so familiar with. The girls moved around the room laughing and leaning out the windows to catcall to men out on the street. Slowly the scene faded until all that could be seen was the guest room, just as it always was . . . with one exception. Looking down at her feet the innkeeper noticed an old-fashioned hairpin. She picked it up absently, putting it in her pocket and reminding herself to make sure the maids did a better job cleaning out the rooms next time.

It would be the first of many hairpins found by the innkeeper, guests and employees of the Union Gables Bed and Breakfast. Eerily they have the habit of appearing just after someone tells a story about the ghostly college girls who are sometimes seen in the inn. Ghosts or no ghosts the Union Gables Bed and Breakfast is a beautifully restored inn, located at 55 Union Street in Saratoga Springs, just minutes up the road from the world famous race track.

Elias Shadwick

In the early 1920s Elias Shadwick was fire chief for Saratoga Springs. He was known for taking on the town politicians and fighting for his department. His support was much needed. The Saratoga Springs fire department was woefully under funded and ill supplied. Many residents lost homes to fire in these early days of the 20th century because of the need their fire department was in. In 1923 the town would lose its only high school to a fire that raged out of control and threatened the buildings around it because the fire department was too far away and too understaffed to get there in time to make a difference.

The loss of the school on Lake Avenue finally drove home the point Elias Shadwick had been trying to make all these years. Public opinion turned in favor of the fire chief and the town fathers followed. Six years after the disastrous fire a brand new ultramodern firehouse was built over the ashes of the high school. Ironically Elias Shadwick would never work in the new fire station he had championed. He died before the new building was complete. But that is not to say that he never got to see the fully equipped fire station. His spirit is said to be there still, watching over the building and the fire fighters who have manned it. No changes have occurred there over the years that haven't been carefully inspected by Elias. Several have described the ghostly presence as a dark shadow. One was awakened in the middle of the night with such a shadow looming over him, as if trying to figure out why he was there. The fire fighter was a long time employee at the station but he and a colleague had switched bunks for the night. Even such a trivial difference in their routine was enough to draw the attention of Saratoga Springs most dedicated fire chief.

The Grand Union Hotel

Ironically, Saratoga Springs most famous ghost has, well, passed on. It disappeared, along with the city's most famous hotel, back in the 1950s but it says something about the power of legend that this spirit is still talked about more than half a century after the last time it was seen.

The Grand Union Hotel was the brainchild of the Capital District's celebrated hotelier, Gideon Putnam. The hotel opened in tandem with the Saratoga Race Course and promptly became the areas premier hotel. It was the luxury enclave of the wealthy elite who traveled to Saratoga to enjoy the summer racing season. It was so popular, in fact, that almost as soon as it opened it underwent a near continuous round of expansion and renovation. Soon, the Grand Union had grown to a staggering 824 rooms, making it the largest hotel in the world at the time.

Sadly the beautiful hotel soon became known for something other than its size and opulence. In 1877 the general manager of the hotel, Judge Henry Hilton, refused rooms to a registered guest and his family. The reason why Hilton barred Joseph Seligman and his family was because they were Jews. While anti-Semitism was certainly nothing new, in the world or the Capital District, this was the first case of its kind to be carried in newspapers around the country. Seligman was an incredibly wealthy international financier and his removal from the guest books at the Grand Union, a hotel he had been a guest of several times before, became a true cause celebre. Controversy over the incident would put the name of the Grand Union Hotel on the tip of everyone's tongue- and certainly not in a good way. Readers of the New York Times were the first to be alerted to the slight, waking up to a front page headline, done entirely in capital letters, that let the world know about 'A SENSATION IN SARATOGA,' which history has gone on to call the Hilton-Seligman Incident.

Both Hilton and Seligman received death threats over the canceled reservation. Hilton stood by his refusal. Even with the bad publicity it generated other hoteliers decided to follow in Hilton's footsteps and declare their own businesses to be Jew free. Jewish groups began extensive boycotts of businesses that embraced the anti-Semitic rules and several large corporations went out of business. This, finally, moved the intractable Hilton. He donated a few thousand dollars to Jewish charities and considered the matter closed. It seemed a paltry measure to many Jewish activists.

At the time Hilton blamed his actions on declining business at the Grand Union Hotel. He had inherited his majority share in the hotel, and apparently some racist sentiments, from Alexander Stewart. Hilton, like Stewart before him, felt that business was lagging at the Grand Union Hotel because 'good' Christians didn't want to stay at a hotel that admitted Jews on the premises. History, however, has given us another possible explanation. Stewart and Seligman had bad blood between them over business and politics. Furthermore Hilton himself would feel that Seligman slighted him, since he was not invited by the businessman to a dinner party attended by then-President Grant. So, the refused reservation could have been due to anti-Semitic sentiments or to a perfectly non-racist, if childish, spat between the men or some combination of the two. Either way, Hilton does not end looking well and his now infamous name only hurried the decline of the once magnificent Grand Union Hotel.

The Grand Union never fully recovered from the bad press. Reservations continued to decline and other newer and even more luxurious hotels sprang up around Saratoga. In time all the hotel would be remembered for was that distasteful Hilton incident, that it had once upon a time been an important hotel, and its ghost.

The ghost was a staple at the hotel. She was said to be a former guest who had committed suicide on the grounds of the hotel. The ghost would appear in a beaded sheath like evening dress and a shock of flaming red hair. The ghost was obviously a wealthy and fashionable young lady and no one could imagine why she had chosen to kill herself while on vacation.

When the Grand Union Hotel was torn down in the 1950s people waited to see if the ghost would appear in the new building that had taken its place. She never has. The last time she was reportedly seen was in the basement of the gutted hotel by construction workers who were working on demolishing the place.

The Country Club Motel

Not all the haunted hotels in Saratoga are rambling hundred-year-old structures. The Country Club Motel, which was located on Route 9 just outside the city itself, was constructed in the 1950s. At the time its rooms were considered to be spacious and modern. Considering its location, just minutes from downtown and directly across the street from the Saratoga Golf and Polo Club, vacancies were rare in the motels early days. But times change and so do peoples perceptions of 'luxury'. It was not long before the rooms at the Country Club Motel seemed cramped and outdated and reservations began to wane. By 2003 the motel closed its doors for good and plans were set in motion to knock the building down and replace it with office space or possibly a shopping plaza. A caretaker was hired to stay on in the motel and protect the property from vandals until the time came when it could be converted into something new.

The caretaker came to heads with the hotels ghost pretty quickly. One day things were normal, if a little lonely, in the abandoned hotel. The next day the caretaker was accosted by the misty visage of a soldier dressed in an old fashioned blue military uniform. It was impossible to make out any features on the spirits face but the uniform was defined enough that the caretaker noticed light glinting off the brass buttons that trailed down the soldier's coat. After this initial meeting the ghost was an almost constant presence. It was seen mostly in and around the basement, a place that thankfully the caretaker almost never had to go, but at least once the figure was seen lurking around the outside of the motel itself.

The spirit made no sense to the caretaker. Historically the closest battle to take place in the area was miles away. But the ghost clung to the building tenaciously through its last months. It was not until official word came that there was a buyer for the property and that the building was slated to be entirely demolished that the ghost was no longer sensed or seen. It was as if, inexplicably, whatever tie he had was to the motel and not the land it sat on and once he knew the motel was ready to go he knew it was time to move on himself.

Schenectady

S chenectady was founded in 1661. Many of the city's old buildings can still be seen in the historic district known as the Stockade. For many years it was known as the 'City that Lights and Hauls the World' and 'Electric City' because it was home to both Thomas Edison's General Electric plant and the American Locomotive Company. G.E is still a large presence in the city today, though many of its manufacturing plants and jobs have been relocated to other parts of the world.

The children's radio performers Big Jon and Sparkie would immortalize the city in the 1950s when they penned a popular song "I Can't Spell Schenectady".

The Visitors

Tourism is big business in New York state. Each year millions of foreign and domestic tourists flock to the state to take in a Broadway show, visit New York's wine country, or enjoy world-class horse racing. With all these visitors perhaps we should not be surprised to hear that New York may have an interstellar reputation as a tourist hotspot as well.

Schenectady is home to one of the more famous U.F.O. sightings in the Capital Region. On April 8, 1956 Raymond Ryan and William Nuff were flying about 6,000 feet above the city of Schenectady, pilot and co-pilot of American Airlines flight 775, when a bright white light blinded them. In that split second instinct took over. Convinced they were about to collide with an oncoming plane Ryan banked his airliner sharply to one side. The oncoming craft mirrored his movement perfectly at the same time he did it. It then turned in an impossibly tight right angle and flew past the plane at an equally impossible thousand miles per hour. There was now no question in Ryan or Nuff's minds that they were not dealing with a typical airplane.

Just as suddenly as the unknown craft picked up speed it dropped. In an instant the craft disappeared from the pilot's line of sight. Surprised, and more than a little unnerved, they flipped on the landing lights to see if they could get a better view of the airspace around them. They were stunned to find the unidentified craft directly in front of their plane. The moment they again turned away from the craft in order to stop colliding midair the strange vehicle began to glow bright orange.

Panicked the pilots radioed the closest air force base to see if they were behind the unusual craft. Things began to get even stranger. The air force base could physically see both the American Airlines flight and a bright orange object but the unidentified craft wasn't showing up on any of their radarscopes.

When relating the story later both pilots confirmed that at this point the air force base told them to pursue the unknown object until they could get some jets in the air that could get a lock on it. Ryan and Nuff did not even have to discuss it before they refused. The air force would deny that they ever told the pilots of the commercial airliner to follow the object, possibly putting their plane full of passengers in jeopardy, but they did begrudgingly admit to seeing some kind of aircraft that they could not identify and that seemed to be capable of maneuvers and speeds far beyond the technology of the times.

Union College

In 1672 Alice Van der Veer was one of the most popular young debutants in the city of Schenectady. She was the only daughter of a wealthy family and stood to someday inherit a great fortune. On top of that she was said to be beautiful, witty, and charming. There wasn't a young man in the city who didn't want to marry her and suitors came from miles away to try their luck at winning her hand. None of them measured up to what her father thought a husband should be for his only daughter.

This is where the history, legend, and hundreds of years old rumors collide. Either Alice fell in love with someone well below her station, or a suitor got a little more aggressive with the young girl than was appropriate for the time, or Father Van der Veer simply over reacted. No matter what the cause the end result was the same. One of Alice's suitors died at the hands of her angry father.

That alone could be enough to start up legends about the Van der Veer family that would survive to this day but the story was not so soon over. The people of Schenectady either had had enough of the city's wealthy elite getting away with whatever they wanted, thought Alice had been something less than the innocent victim in the affair, or thought her father had completely over reacted. An angry mob started to march, torches and pitchforks in hand, on the Van der Veer mansion. As they walked the mob grew, as mobs tend to do. By the time they reached the grounds of the home the mob was said to be hundreds strong.

Once a year the spirit of a young woman is seen walking thorugh these gates on her way to Jackson's Garden.

Legend tells us that Alice and her father were pulled from the home and burned at the stake. It seems more likely that their house was torched and father and daughter, too scared to leave their home and face the mob, perished within. Either way both died and a ghost story was begun.

The ghostly figure of Alice Van der Veer can be seen on the first full moon of the summer, presumably the same as the night she died. She comes from the direction of the Stockade and floats calmly across the grounds of Union College until she reaches Jackson's Garden, which is thought to cover the land where she burned to death. She has sometimes been blamed for freak unexplained power outages but over all she is a harmless specter.

The beautiful Union College campus is built on the same land where and angry mob killed a young debutant and her father in the 1600s.

Neighborly

In 1975 Marybeth Tinning arrived at St. Claire's Hospital clutching her unresponsive five-month-old baby. She told the emergency room nurse she and baby had been driving around Schenectady when she noticed he wasn't breathing. The little boy, Nathan, was pronounced dead on arrival. The doctors could find no reason why the child would have stopped breathing but there was also no evidence of foul play. The oddest thing about the tragedy was that Nathan was the fifth child of Marybeth Tinning to die of unexplainable causes in just four years. The first four children had also died young, all between the ages of three weeks to four years. The first daughter appeared to die from disease, but each one after her had stopped breathing for no reason doctors could find.

For three years the Tinnings remained childless and the general feeling among their neighbors was that they had finally given up on the idea of children after all their heartache. But in 1978 the Tinning's started adoption proceedings. Shortly before they welcomed their adopted son into their home, Marybeth found out she was pregnant for her sixth time. After all their losses it seemed things were looking up for them, and they decided to continue on with the adoption. Their adopted child arrived just two months before Marybeth gave birth to her sixth child. But the Tinning luck did not seem to have turned. Shortly after the birth of their new daughter, Mary Frances, Marybeth was back in the emergency room saying the baby had been having seizures and stopped breathing. The hospital staff was able to resuscitate the child and sent her home. A month later Marybeth and Mary Frances were back in the same emergency room. Marybeth had, she said, found the child in her crib and not breathing. The child was, this time, brain dead and died soon after reaching the hospital.

The Tinning's troubles were chalked up to a failure to thrive, caused by a previously unknown genetic disorder. Genetics, of course, were not well understood in the 1970s. But with six mysteriously dead children and no signs of abuse it seemed it could be the only cause. The general feeling at that time in the neighborhood was that the Tinning's should enjoy their adopted child and consider him a blessing.

But Marybeth Tinning was soon pregnant again. And again, soon after the child's birth, she was rushing an unconscious baby to the emergency located conveniently across the street from her apartment. Again no cause could be found and the child was sent home. A few days later, unsurprisingly, the child was dead. One would think, at this point, that there were be rumors of something a little more sinister going on at the Tinning apartment than bad genes and bad luck. However, if anything was said, it was not said loudly or by many. Neighbors turned out in droves to comfort Marybeth Tinning. Talk really did not start at all until 1981 when Marybeth Tinning showed up at her pediatrician's office with her adopted child unconscious and wrapped in a blanket. Marybeth swore she didn't know what could have happened to the child. She discovered him in his bed unconscious and could not wake him. The doctor quickly determined the child, like all of Marybeth's biological children before him, was dead.

In hindsight it is hard to tell why things were allowed to go on as long as they had. Incredibly even the death of an adopted child was not enough to cause authorities to take a harder look what might be happening in the Tinning apartment. Every child in Marybeth's care, from her own biological children to an adopted son, stopped breathing and died mysteriously, and every time it happened they were alone with her. It actually took the birth, and eventual death, of a ninth child before a police investigation caused Marybeth to confess to smothering three of her children. It was a confession she later recanted.

A jury took little stock in Marybeth's assertion that the police coerced her into a confession. In 1987 a jury of her peers would find her guilty of second-degree murder. Marybeth Tinning was only ever convicted in the death of her last child, Tami Lynne. The police didn't have enough evidence after so many years had passed to try her for the deaths of any of her other children. The court of popular opinion is not so lenient.

The case was, needless to say, a sensation. It made police and hospital workers look negligent. It made neighbors look detached and uninvolved. But of course the real question of everyone's mind was "What could drive a mother to do such a thing?" Marybeth seems to have been nearly addicted to the attention she received with each pregnancy and each tragic death that followed. Neighbors said she loved to flaunt her pregnancy, long before she was visibly showing she would wear maternity clothes to draw attention to her condition. And with each death the wave of sympathy for Marybeth grew. She was a well known, if pitied, figure in her Schenectady neighborhood.

The legacy of Marybeth Tinning lives on today in the same neighborhood where all nine of her children met their untimely deaths. You can find many people, most too young to have even been alive during the Tinning's time in Schenectady, who can easily point out the house they rented an apartment in. You can find even more who will swear up and down that the murderous ghost of Marybeth still stalks the neighborhood looking for children. However, that would be quite a feat for Marybeth's spirit considering that the woman is very much alive and well, and still incarcerated, in the Bedford Hills Correctional Facility, located a two and a half hour drive away from her former Schenectady apartment.

So much attention is paid to the entirely legendary ghost of Marybeth that few people realize there is a haunted house just two houses away from the former apartment of the Tinning's. Schenectady is known for its two family homes. In Marybeth's old neighborhood you'll find streets full of nearly identical duplexes. Each one has an upstairs apartment and a matching downstairs, each floor with a similar floor plan, the same as the buildings on either side of it, and usually with a porch for each floor facing the street. They have narrow staircases to the second floor, a small landing outside the entry doors, and good-sized living and dining rooms. One small bedroom opens up off of the dining room, the other small bedroom can be found off the small kitchen in the back of the house. These are long narrow buildings, stretching back to tiny backyard, if they are lucky, and separated from each other by just a narrow driveway. Often the only difference between any of the houses on the street is the color of their siding and how good of repair the apartment building is in.

Many young couples in Schenectady get their start in these very common types of residences. Tara and Leo were no different. Shortly after their wedding they were, like so many of their friends before them, lugging their furniture up the narrow stairs to the top floor of one of these Schenectady duplexes. Caught up with moving, switching the electricity over to their name, getting phone service, and all of the many trivialities that come with moving into a new home they didn't give much thought to the downstairs neighbor. After a few days of lugging couches into place and dropping oversized boxes on the uncarpeted floors Tara waited anxiously to see if the downstairs neighbor would complain. But when she realized no one was running up the stairs to knock at their door, the police never showed up saying they got a call, and the landlord seemed pleased with his new tenants she realized that whomever was downstairs they didn't seem to mind the noise very much- or maybe they were just use to getting new neighbors.

Leo and Tara quickly settled into the rhythm of the new house. Slowly their belongings were unpacked and the apartment started to feel like a true home to them. The people on either side of their building were very friendly, offering to help carry things upstairs for them, and letting them know who on the street was trouble and who wasn't. A few times when Leo came up onto the porch, checking the mailbox before coming inside, he would see an old woman peering at him from between the curtains in the downstairs window. At first he waved, hoping he looked friendly and not intimidating. But each time the curtain would drop back in place and he'd see no more of their elusive downstairs neighbor. Leo passed it off. It wasn't always the safest neighborhood and it was probably scary for an old woman to have new neighbors she knew nothing about.

Tara seemed more curious about the old woman downstairs. "I never hear her leave," She told him one night at dinner.

"She might not get around so easily. She looks pretty old from what I've seen of her," Leo said.

"How does she go to the doctor than? They don't make house calls."

"Hon," Leo told her. "A lot of these old people are on fixed incomes. They don't go to the doctor until they really have to go to the doctor."

Tara wasn't mollified. "What about the grocery store? Everybody has to eat."

Leo didn't have a quick answer for that one. It seemed obvious to him though that Tara wasn't in the apartment all the time. The lady downstairs could easily be having food dropped off by a local church or one of her children. They wouldn't necessarily know about it.

Tara was not so easily convinced. There were two lessons Tara had been taught at an early age. The first was that being neighborly was important. The second was that no one turned down free food. So, a few days later she was downstairs knocking politely at the neighbor's door with one hand while balancing a casserole in the other. She knocked and knocked, the knocks getting increasingly louder just in case the old woman was hard of hearing, but no matter how hard she banged on the door no one came to answer it. Now Tara wasn't just concerned, she was slighted. Leo told her to leave the poor woman alone and promptly forgot about the whole thing.

Months went by and in time Leo and Tara only thought of the woman at all if they happened to catch one of her sneaky looks from behind the lace curtains. The situation might have gone on indefinitely except that winter the heat mysteriously stopped working. One call to the landlord and he was out immediately checking pipes and climbing around the basement furnace with Leo. After a few hours of fiddling around they got things going again. They were standing at the front door chatting, saying their good byes, when something occurred to Leo.

"Are you going to go in and explain what happened to the neighbor'? He asked.

The landlord gave him a puzzled look. When he realized it wasn't some kind of joke he informed Leo that they didn't have a downstairs neighbor. Incredulous Leo told him about the months of seeing the old woman peering out at them when they were on the porch. Now the landlord was really concerned. The last tenant had moved out right before Leo and Tara had moved in upstairs. The landlord normally would have been trying to rent the place out immediately after getting it painted but he'd held off this time. His daughter would be eighteen soon and had mentioned a few times she'd like to live in the apartment so he figured it would be better to wait and see what she decided than to get tenants he'd have to try and get rid of a few months down the road. Could someone have been living illegally in the apartment all this time?

A little old lady didn't sound like much to be worried about but figuring that these days you just didn't know about people he asked Leo to come check the place out with him. Inside they found the apartment clearly empty and everything covered in dust. If anyone had been using the apartment their footprints would have shown up clearly. From inside Leo saw that the curtains that looked like bright white lace from the outside were so old and dusty he worried they'd fall to pieces if he tried touching them to peer outside as he'd been spied on so often during the past few months. Leo and the landlord decided to pass it off as a trick of the light since it was so obvious the apartment has been unused for a long time.

Leo and Tara didn't see the old woman again but a few months later they did get a new neighbor. The landlord's daughter did end up moving downstairs and she liked to tell the couple about the ghostly occurrences she sometimes experienced inside the apartment.

A Not-so-friendly Warning

Jennifer Stevens, a lifelong Schenectady resident, could have told Pilots Ryan and Nuff they got off easy- very easy. Jennifer was extremely interested in U.F.O. sightings and, until 1968, was probably the single most active U.F.O investigator in the Capital Region. Starting early in 1968 Jenifer began to receive strange phone calls and have even stranger problems with her home telephone. After complaining several times the phone company did their own investigation and could never explain what the cause of the problems was.

Around the same time that the phone company began their investigations Jennifer's husband Peter was accosted by two men in black suits who warned him that he better put a stop to his wife's U.F.O hobby. Unnerved by the experience Peter Stevens did a quick sketch of the men who had threatened him. Later on another U.F.O investigator, John Keel, would see the sketch and declare it a perfect match for the so-called 'men in black'.

Peter wouldn't live to hear this declaration. Shortly after his run in with the strange men he died unexpectedly. Official reports blamed his death on a vague medical condition but his wife was convinced that it was caused by the men in black in order to make her stop her research.

Vale Cemetery

Most of the haunting in this State Street cemetery seems to center in and around an old church like building in the cemetery. Strange figures can be seen both inside and outside the building, as if drawn there. Some have been seen passing directly thorough the walls in order to get inside. Sometimes at night unearthly glows and strange colors have been seen coming from the windows and there is a sound of many voices raised in song.

The grounds of Veil Cemetery are nearly as haunted as the church. The statuary here is sometimes heard crying out at night, in sadness or in pain, and you can find many witnesses who swear they have seen blood pour from the statues eyes. Many apparitions have been seen, alone and in groups, floating amongst the tombstones and even relaxing in the cemetery trees.

The Stockade

The Stockade Historic District is a unique look into the early history of the Capital Region. It is the oldest neighborhood in Schenectady, and some consider it the oldest and most well preserved neighborhood in the country. It contains many historic buildings from the 17th, 18th, and 19th centuries. The neighborhoods oldest home dates from 1690. This has been a protected area since the 1960's when much money and effort was poured into the restoration of the areas oldest homes and strict building codes were enacted to protect and preserve all of the buildings in the area. The National Parks Service has said the Stockade neighborhood contains the highest concentration of period homes in the entire country.

And, of course, any area infused with as much history and as many old buildings as the Stockade is thought to have more than a couple ghosts lingering about its narrow tree lined streets and carefully restored homes.

The Dutch Reformed Church is a stockade landmark. It sits directly across the street from the very haunted Stockade Inn.

The Front Street Apartment

Jessica was warned about the ghost before she ever even moved into the Front Street apartment. In her initial meeting with the landlord he warned her that he went through tenants very quickly. Taken aback by his candor she asked why, figuring it was a joke or something.

"They don't care for our ghost, I guess." He said, watching carefully for her reaction to this admission.

Jess started to laugh . . . and then by the look on his face realized he was *not* joking. Calmly, a little pityingly, she informed him that she did not believe in ghosts.

"That's what they all say, until they move out". He told her, sighing resignedly.

As frank as the landlord was the other tenants in the building were even more forthcoming. Jess hadn't even finished carrying her things upstairs before two different tenants popped in to say hi . . . and give her a heads up that the building was haunted. They too seemed unimpressed when she said that she did not believe in ghosts. By the time a third neighbor came by she was done protesting and, trying to make polite conversation more than anything else, asked if he knew who the ghost was supposed to be or why they were haunting the building.

"Well," said the neighbor, a guy about her age that lived across the hall, "no one knows for sure but there's an old forgotten Indian burial ground in the backyard, so I think that has something to do with it. There are probably all kinds of graves back there!"

"Where?" Asked Jess, exasperated, motioning out the window towards the postage stamp sized backyard that was barely big enough to contain the trashcans and recycling bins for the four apartments.

While a Native American burial ground seems unlikely, the stuff of urban legends that does not take into consideration the fact that the annual floods that plague the Stockade each spring would have discouraged any burial grounds or at least uncovered any that were there, it soon became apparent to even an unbeliever like Jessica that something peculiar was going on in the building. Doors would open and shut by themselves, and would be followed by the feeling of an invisible presence in the room. Doors that won't remain still are a common complaint in old houses- but even locked doors were not immune in Jessica's new apartment. Often she would feel tugs at her clothing and at night her blankets were yanked off of her with sudden violent speed.

One night, after the covers had been ripped off of her five or six times, Jess got fed up. Grabbing them off the floor she pulled the blankets over herself and clutched the edge as tightly as she could. Several minutes later the covers were nearly jerked from her hands. Gritting her teeth Jess clung to them. The unseen force continued to try and pull the covers from her grip. Jess tugged back. She lay there frozen, realizing she was locked in a tug of war with something she could not even see. After a few moments the ghost gave up and, hoping that was the end of it, Jess fell into a troubled slumber.

If Jess had thought that the ghost was going to leave her alone now that she had stood up to it she quickly learned otherwise. First thing in the morning her cabinet doors were slamming and, for the first time, she found her things the apartment strewn about. While the tugs at her clothing had been playful, if inexplicable, before now they were threatening. A few times she felt pinches from unseen hands. The apartment was suddenly plagued with cold spots and no matter how high she turned up the temperature she couldn't get warm. Other people in the building told her that previous tenants who had complained about the ghost seemed to become its focus. This seemed to be what was happening to Jessica now.

Within a few weeks Jess couldn't take it any more. Like so many tenants before her she called the landlord and told him she was ready tomove out. It seemed as if her decision pleased the spirit. Her last month there was the quietest time she had spent in the apartment. The pinches stopped and she was no longer awakened at night.

The Stockade Inn

The Stockade Inn, on North Church Street, offers fine dining, private function rooms and fourteen careful restored hotel rooms spread over three floors. It started life as a bank in the 1800s. Banking occurred on the first floor while the upper floors served as a residence for the bank manager. From the 1850s to the beginning of the 1900s the building went from being a bank to a private residence to a high school. In 1904 the building passed into the hands of The Mohawk Club, a private gentlemen's club where Schenectady's political leaders and most important business could spend the evenings smoking cigars, sipping fine brandies, and schmoozing with one another.

As soon as the Mohawk Club took over employees started complaining about the ghosts. The most widely reported spirit was that of a well dressed gentleman who seemed to linger around the second floor billiards room. This spirit looked solid enough, and was dressed like an upper class gentleman of the times, so it was often mistaken for one of the clubs members. Many people did not even realize what they were seeing was a ghost until they walked up to introduce themselves and the man disappeared right before their eyes or turned and walked through the wall behind him.

Employees quickly found that this was not the only ghost walking the hallways of the Mohawk Club. In the kitchens a playful force slammed cabinets and hid utensils that had been in plain sight on the counters only moments before. When the kitchen ghost was feeling especially active it was known for flinging items from the cabinets after banging the doors open. At least one employee quit their well paying job at the Mohawk Club because they couldn't stand dodging flying plates thrown at them by unseen hands.

The Stockade Inn offers lodging, fine dinning, banquet halls and many ghosts.

The Mohawk Club kept lodging rooms for members and associates. It was not uncommon for guests staying in the third floor rooms to leave hastily in the middle of the night. The few who stopped long enough to explain their hasty departures made vague complaints about bad smells or banging noises that employees never heard or smelled themselves.

The building on the corner of Union and North Church Street became the Stockade Inn in 2003. The resident ghosts introduced themselves to the new owners long before the Inn ever opened its doors. Construction workers, tasked with returning the building to its former glory, griped about strange noises on the third floor, just like the lodgers in days gone by. Tools left for a minute on the second and third floors had a reputation for disappearing, never to be seen again.

Despite the missing tools the Stockade Inn opened with the front desk phone ringing off the hook. Excited clerks answered the phones expecting to book rooms and make reservations for the restaurant. Instead their excitement turned to confusion. There was no one on the other end of the phone. Figuring there was a problem with the phones they checked the board a little closer. The calls were coming from the empty rooms above them!

Right around the time the front desk clerks realized the oddity with the phone calls *another* phone in the lobby started to ring. This one no one wanted to answer- since it was an antique phone that had just been placed there for decoration and was not connected to the phone lines at all! After the first day the front desk never received calls from empty rooms upstairs again and no one was able to offer a scientific explanation for why it had happened in the first place. But for weeks, every so often, the disconnected antique phone in the lobby would ring. Eventually it was removed.

Some of the ghosts at the Stockade Inn have been
reported for over a hundred years.

Since the 2003 opening guests and employees have reported seeing the very same specters that members of the Mohawk Club reported seeing close to a hundred years before. It is impossible to know what the ghosts think of the changes they've witnessed over the years but one can't help but think they feel at home in the carefully restored, elegant Stockade Inn.

Ghosts of the Schenectady Massacre

As the original building site of the city of Schenectady the Stockade area was once, well, surrounded by a heavily fortified stockade. This was meant to be a defensive measure but unfortunately when the time came it did little to help the early inhabitants.

The danger was not so much from the local Native Americans themselves as it was from the outside influences acting upon the local tribes. The English were supplying weapons to the Iroquois, who then used those weapons in a long series of successful raids against the Sault and Algonquin tribes living in and around French settlements to the north. When the French and their own local Native populations decided it was time to even the score they headed south towards Fort Orange, which in present day is Albany.

But things were running smoothly at Fort Orange, it was well manned, well equipped, and fully stocked to survive a long siege. Scouts soon found the opposite to be true at the Schenectady Stockade though. A split decision turned the massed troops towards the thriving settlement.

They attacked in the dead of night in frigid February weather. The Stockade was, indeed, defenseless. Most residents were asleep and did not have time to arm themselves to fight back. Men sent wives and small children out into the snowy night wearing just their flimsy pajamas and without shoes to flee the settlement and hide in the woods, they were to try and make it to the safety of Fort Orange in Albany if they could. By morning over sixty buildings in the settlement were burned and as many residents were dead. The French and Native troops took nearly thirty prisoners and twice as many horses as the spoils of war.

The raid was devastating to the small community. In the end it is nearly impossible to get an accurate death count from that one night. How many children wandered into the woods and were not seen again? How many people starved or fell to disease from malnutrition because the stores they had set aside to last till spring had been destroyed? But even in the midst of ruin there were heroes. The founding family of Scotia, the settlement directly across the river from the Stockade, had long been allies of the French. They used their connection to claim rights to a number of prisoners, telling the French that great numbers of strangers were their close relatives and they wanted them returned unharmed. They took back as many prisoners as they could.

This statue, known as Laurence the Indian around the Stockade, sits in the heart of the oldest section of the district at the intersections of Front, Green, and North Ferry Streets. It is directly across the street from Arthurs Market, which has been a Stockade landmark since 1795.

It has long been known that traumatic events can cause re-verberations long after they've finished in the form of haunting. The Schenectady Massacre is no exception. Sometimes late at night, figures in old-fashioned bedclothes can be seen running up and down the narrow old streets of the Stockade. Sometimes it is even possible to get a glimpse of those pursuing the frightened residents. Quite often a team of ghostly horses, frothing at the mouth and with a wild look in their eyes, are seen racing up the street in a frightened group. It seems that even all of these years later they are fleeing the burning barn they escaped from. Even when the horses themselves are not visible it is possible to hear the frantic thunder of their hooves on the street.

Front Street is sometimes traveled by ghostly horses dating back to the Schenectady Massacre.

Scotia

Glen Sanders Mansion

Ask most Scotians who Glen Sanders was and they'll tell you he was the guy who built the first house in Scotia, a house that is still standing today. It's an easy mistake to make. While the home has been known as the Glen Sanders Mansion, or Glen Sanders Estate, since 1765 it would be more properly called Glen-Sanders. This is because Glen Sanders never existed. The name actually comes from two distinguished Capital District families who became forever tied together by marriage in the mid 1770s.

The original Glen mansion dating from 1658 no longer exists. Alexander Glen built the massive stone house a few years before the founding of the cities of Schenectady or Scotia and was unaware of the yearly flooding that occurs around the Mohawk River each spring. That is to say that Alexander Glen built his house a few hundred feet closer to the banks of the river than he should have. Even his enormous stone goliath of a house was not able to withstand the river waters. When he rebuilt he would move the house considerably further up the hill from the river and while the Mohawk may have come close to the homes foundations in particularly severe floods it has never managed to destroy the replacement Glen home the way it did the first.

This second Glen home, despite Alexander Glen being a wealthy agent for the Dutch West India Company, was far more modest a structure than either the first house or the one that stands today. Alexander, one can't help but think, wasn't going to take any more chances building something extravagant just for the Mohawk to claim it again. The second Glen House was, originally, just one room. Under Alexander's cautious care, in time, a hall and two others would be added to that one room.

The original Glen House, built in the 1600s, was lost to flooding. Glen Sanders Mansion was built using materials from the first house.

It was not until Alexander's son Johannes inherited the house that it would become anything like what it is today. He tacked another wing onto his father's modest four-room house and soon garnered a reputation for being a generous host. Louis Philippe of France would stay here through much of his exile. The home, and the Glen family, would play an important part in the history of the Capital District. Alexander Glen, a close friend to the Native population, would hide and save a Jesuit priest the local Iroquois tribe asked him to lock up for the night before they executed him. John Glen would prove instrumental in saving dozens of survivors of the Schenectady Massacre, George Washington was a frequent guest in the house, and even in modern days the home boasted a cannonball lodged in one wall.

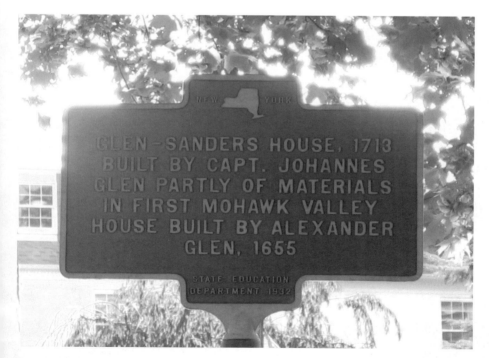

The Glen House was visited by important figures of their day, such as George Washington. Today their home is a restaurant, inn, and banquet hall.

In 1769 Alexander Glen's great-granddaughter inherited the home. Just a few years earlier she had married John Sanders of Albany. From this time on the home would forever be known as the Glen Sanders House. The home would continue to be passed down through the line of Debra and Johns descendants until the 1960s. In 1998 restaurateur Angelo Mazzone purchased it. He would heavily renovate the house, a move that was controversial in some quarters, and add on another wing. Today Glen Sanders Mansion is a fine dining establishment, banquet hall, and inn. The original single room that Alexander Glen built in the 1600s is used as a kitchen and many of the Glen's original belongings and furniture are still in use in the house.

The Glen Sanders Mansion, as it is today.

The oldest parts of the house are said to heavily haunted. A few of the ghosts even seem to confirm some of the rumors that have long been associated with the Glen House. Located across the street from the Glen Sanders Mansion is the Scotia branch of the Schenectady Public Library. It was known as the Abraham Glen house, Abraham being a Glen relative. There are many reports of an underground tunnel connecting the Glen Mansion with Abrahams' home and there has been some speculation that it was used as a northern branch of the Underground Railroad, to help transport escaped slaves to Canada, rather than simply just a tunnel used to help transport food supplies and goods between the two houses in poor weather. The tunnel has been rumored to be sealed totally or to be in such poor repair that it's not considered safe to explore it so no one has been able to confirm its supposed link with the Underground Railroad. But a psychic who visited the Glen Sanders Mansion recently said she saw very clearly three Black young adults sneaking down the backstairs of the Mansion. They were, the psychic sensed, very afraid of being detected. Could these be the spirits of escaped slaves who stayed for a while in the Glen Sanders Mansion while on their way to freedom? Or were they simply former servants of the Glens themselves who were afraid of being caught for some other reason?

Debra Sanders is the most famous of the ghosts at Glen Sanders Mansion. Appropriately enough she haunts the dining room that is named after her. This room is covered in murals depicting the house and grounds as they would have been during Debra's day. Even all these years after her death she continues the Glen tradition of being a gracious hostess. Many sensitive people have described feeling her calming and welcoming presence in the room. A few employees claim that over the years they have often found knick-knacks and other items that once belonged to Debra herself moved from their various resting spots around the house and littered around this room.

This building use to belong to a Glen relative, today it is the Scotia Public Library. An underground tunnel connects the library with Glen Sanders Mansion.

The Stockade Room is also well haunted though by less identifiable spirits. In recent years the Mansion has opened itself up to ghost hunters and local media interested in gathering information about the homes spirits. This room inevitably reveals dozens of orbs in photographs taken here and EVPs have shown surprisingly vocal results.

The basement of Glen Sanders Mansion seems to be heavily haunted. Many employees refuse to go down there at all. Those that have in the course of their duties at the Mansion report flickering lights, not terribly strange in such an old house, but even flashlights turn on and off at whim.

The Men in Black

The men in black are phenomena all their own that is most often associated with U.F.O sightings and various government or alien conspiracy theories. They first came to the attention of popular culture in the 1950s and 1960s but stories about men in black have been reported since then.

They normally appear to those who have, outspokenly, claimed to have seen a U.F.O or had an alien abduction experience. They arrive in black cars and are usually, as the name implies, dressed in generic black suits and wearing dark sunglasses. The men in black proceed to tell the U.F.O witness intimate details about their day to life, as if that person has long been under surveillance of some type. It is rare for the men in black to specifically identify themselves as belonging to any kind of governmental body but those who encounter them always feel that is what they are implying. Some flash badges to quick to be seen clearly or, if they are seen, that are unidentifiable with any known authorities. After letting the person know how much is known about them, where they work, their loved ones, their day to day routines, the men in black offer up vague threats that are usually enough to keep the person from pursuing bringing attention to their alien encounter.

If that was all there was to the men in black it would be easy to pass them off as some kind of shadowy government agency whose mission is to keep information about true alien encounters quiet for some reason only the Federal government knows. But the men in black often exhibit extremely unusual behavior. Oftentimes the black car they drive up in is many decades old, even though it appears brand new. A few times they have confronted car buffs who later on swear that while the car looked vaguely old fashioned it was of no make or model they have ever encountered before. Sometimes the men in black are wearing equally old-fashioned dark suits though they rarely manage to coordinate the right time periods for both their car and their fashion. They may appear in impeccable black suits but wearing no shoes, or with their shoes on the wrong feet. Furthermore the men in black often seemed flummoxed by even the most common electronic devices, as if cell phones or doorbells are something they've never encountered before. On the other hand there are an almost equal number of reported incidents where the men in black were said to have technologies that were completely unrecognizable and seemed to be far advanced beyond anything currently on the market.

The men in black are not always dressed in black. The term is a generic one that applies to any oddly behaving, and vaguely threatening, unexplained figure that shows up after an alien encounter. They tend to travel in groups of three and are known for being short and having a swarthy skin color. Of course there is nothing definite when it comes to men in black. A very few witnesses have reported their MIB were of incredible height, seven or eight feet. A small handful of witnesses have said they've seen wires traveling in and out of the skin of the men in black when a pant leg or jacket sleeve has accidentally pulled up. The MIBs invariably wear dark sunglasses and, since some witnesses claim to have seen mechanical glowing and flashing lights where their eyes should be, it is thought the glasses are meant to hide this disturbing aspect of their appearance.

Everyone has their own theory as to who the men in black are. Many feel that they are part of a covert governmental agency whose mission is to stop legitimate alien encounters from making news. Other people feel that the men in black are aliens themselves, which would explain their unfamiliarity with Earth customs and technology, but not why aliens would make themselves known to humans just to threaten them into silence later. Other popular, and outlandish, theories say the men in black are cyborgs possibly created by aliens, or time travelers, or alien human hybrids intent on keeping the existence of aliens quiet so they themselves won't be the subject of discrimination. One of the more out-there schools of thought associates the MIBs with demon encounters from days of old. This school of thought seems to be evenly split between believing that the men in black are actual demons, who have tried to modernize their appearance to blend in better with society, or believing that the men in black have always appeared throughout history (being aliens or time travelers) and that ancient man interpreted their strange dress and habits as demonic in nature.

For four years, in the late 1960s and early 1970s, many Scotia residents reported men in black. Because of their threatening nature, it is likely that many more people were visited than ever spoke up about their encounters. The visits began just weeks after there were a multitude of U.F.O sightings along the Mohawk River. Peggy, a Scotia resident who lived on a street facing the river, described seeing a large star fall and then begin to shoot around the night sky at a fast speed and at impossible angles. She and her neighbors watched the phenomenon for some time before the strange light shot a baseball sized object out over their heads. In the weeks that followed Peggy would see a lot of strange things around her house and work. Her home was suddenly haunted, something Peggy never believed in before or had ever sensed about her own residence. The ghostly figure of a man walked from room to room. Her cat began to chase something unseen around the house for hours at a time until the poor animal dropped, exhausted.

Her workplace was no respite from the strange incidents that had started to follow her wherever she went. Shortly after the first U.F.O sighting, she began a new job. On her first day, a large security guard accosted her. The security guard cornered Peggy and started to tell her about his involvement with a top-secret organization. Luckily for the frightened woman a co-worker overheard the exchange and interrupted, telling the guard he was crazy and leading Peggy away from him. Both Peggy and her new co-worker saw something strange flicker in the guards' eyes, something they both later described as beams of light. Two days later the guard walked off the job and was never seen again.

For several months Scotia residents saw unidentifiable spacecraft flying above the Mohawk River.

Meanwhile other Scotia residents were also seeing U.F.O.s in the sky above the river at night and the more vocal of them were receiving visits from men in black. One lady even had a pet dragged away from her yard by what she would later describe as 'little men'. The sightings of colored lights and unidentifiable spacecraft continued sporadically for months. That winter two separate witnesses would call in reports that they were seeing some kind of craft hovering very low above the frozen river right near a teenaged boy who was apparently using the frozen river as a shortcut home. The next day a teenager's body would be found on the frozen river. Officially the boy died of exposure but some people said his footprints showed he had been running along the riverbed and that his final few steps made it appear that he had been dragged.

The multitude of reports over such a long period of time drew many U.F.O hobbyists from around the country. Even they were not immune to the threats from the MIBs. Three men who told them, very blandly, that "People who look for U.F.O's should be very, very careful", stopped two U.F.O researchers in a coffee shop. The men said a blue Lincoln followed them around for weeks and that when they returned home they found the same car parked outside their residences.

Eventually sightings of strange aircraft stopped but visits from men in black were rumored to go on for another three years. There have been famous U.F.O sightings in the Capital District since then, but none have been followed by the flurry of men in black activity afterwards like the Scotia incident.

The New House

When Jane bought the 1800's farmhouse on the outskirts of Scotia it was in need of some TLC. Luckily her husband was a capable carpenter, having worked alongside his own father in a family owned construction business for years. Sadly her father in law would never get the chance to pound a few nails in at their new home. Right around the time they bought the property his heart condition worsened and he died within a few days of the closing.

Obviously saddened Jane and her husband tried to take some joy in their new home. One morning while her husband was out buying lumber Jane stood at the kitchen sink washing dishes and staring out into the small backyard. Behind her she heard the sounds of a man's heavy footsteps walking down the stairs. Jane turned quickly, nearly dropped the dish she was washing- she *knew* she was alone in the house. Standing there on the stairs leading from the first to second floor was her father in law. He stood there for just a second and then turned and walked upstairs, each step of his heavy workbooks clunking soundly on the stairs. Jane raced through the kitchen and dashed up the stairs, hoping to communicate with the spirit, but he was gone.

Jane's husband couldn't understand why his father's spirit had revealed itself to her and not him. Jane couldn't help but feel that he had only come by to check out the new house.

Stillwater

Stillwater Cemetery

S tillwater Cemetery is notorious for an oversized glowing green orb that is sometimes spotted above the tombstones. It has been seen by both the naked eye and has been caught on camera in photographs. The orb doesn't seem to be linked to any one grave in particular and local paranormal buffs have tried to figure out if there is some kind of significance to why it is sometimes above one tombstone as opposed to another, at any given time. As of yet no good theories have come forward.

What is less well known about the Stillwater Cemetery is that it is a great place to pick up EVPs. EVP stands for electronic voice phenomena. EVP's are unexplainable voices and sounds that are captured by recording equipment even though they were inaudible at the time of the recording. An EVP can be a voice that appears on recordings of unoccupied rooms or even voices that seem to manifest out of the white noise sounds of electrical appliances such as the static on a television or the hum of a fan.

Historically EVP's appeared as soon as there was recording equipment available to capture them. People have always been interested in 'proving' there is life after death. Using modern technologies as always been seen as making these efforts more scientific and as a way of differentiating the serious paranormal investigator from the more New Age type of ghost hunter. The legitimate scientific community has always been quick to distance themselves from any of these attempts. Even people who believe in the extraordinary nature of EVP's don't always agree that ghosts cause them. People have proposed that EVP's are caused by everything from alien transmissions to being evidence of a kind of unconscious telepathy. Almost as many people will tell you that EVPs are proof of psychic powers as they are proof that the spirits of the dearly departed are trying to communicate with the living. Some of the more outlandish theories that have been linked to EVP's only work to make the scientific community want to distance themselves even more from the phenomena. The leading explanation from the scientific community is that the messages heard in EVPs are nothing more than what the listener wants to hear, that they are the subconscious's way of making itself known.

The earliest known publicized EVP's were made by photographer Attila von Szalay who in the 1950's experimented with several different ways of tuning into the frequencies of the dead. Von Szalay tried a variety of different techniques, everything from record players to equipment he built himself that involved a sound proofed cabinet with a recording device inside. Using these various techniques Von Szalay managed to record such 'otherworldly' message as "Hot Dog, Art!" and "Merry Christmas to you all!". As silly as these spirit messages seem Von Szalay wrote several articles, that would go on to be published by a variety of at least half way respectable journals, and was lauded for applying scientific methods to an area of thought that had previously been dominated by cheats and charlatans. His journalistic success garnered him a book contract that resulted in him co-authoring a book on the subject of EVP's.

Believe it or not, Von Szalay's messages are a little easier to swallow as true accounts of communing with the dead then some of the other more famous recordings. In the early 1980's William O'Neil, a famous stockbroker, held a press conference where he announced he had created an audio device that allowed the living to converse easily with the dead. O'Neil took no credit for the invention, attributing its design to a scientist that had died half a dozen years earlier. O'Neil, it was announced, had been transmitted the design psychically. At this press conference O'Neil offered, for free, to give the instructions on how to build a similar 'Spiricom' to any researchers who were interested in verifying his claims. Unfortunately no other researcher was able to get the results from their Spiricoms that O'Neil had claimed to get from his. He was dismissed as a fraud, or possibly as being mentally unstable, but a few stalwart supporters felt that O'Neil's success with the device was linked to some sort of high level of psychic ability that he possessed that was lacking in every other Spiricom user.

With all of these unusual claims it is no surprise that EVP's are largely ignored by the mainstream scientific community. However, anyone who actually captures one of these recordings or listens to one will be hard pressed to explain them away easily. The voices are, most often, indistinct and hard to understand, as if coming across to the listener over long distances. It is not unusual for each syllable to sound as though it is being said at vastly different speeds. Many times the voices recorded will respond to questions being spoken by the living people in the room- even if those people heard no voices at the time of the recording! But most often EVP's are normally very brief, a single word or short phrase, that have no connection to anything going on in the world of the living.

Even those who think EVPs are utter rubbish agree to be very careful with them. If they are messages from your own subconscious, there is usually a reason why these feelings have been buried there. The listener may not be ready to consciously confront these thoughts. If they are messages from the dead they are not to be depended on. You have no way of knowing if the voice you've recorded is of a loved one trying to pass you an important message, or a spectral jokester with an agenda of their own. In many cases it seems the voices are not even trying to directly communicate with the living and that the recording has simply picked up on a conversation between groups of spirits that has nothing at all to do with the world of the living. Interestingly the most common EVP captured is the sound of a barking dog. Some people have not only captured the pet but also what seems to be the voice of its master issuing it commands to sit, to speak, and sometimes to please stop all that barking!

The 2005 movie *White Noise*, whose plot centers around EVP's, chillingly ends with the warning that every 1 in 12 EVP recordings are threatening in nature. It is unclear where the filmmakers got this 'fact' and many experts in the field of parapsychology have publicly disputed the numbers. But just because the statistics is wrong doesn't mean the sentiment is wrong, too. A big part of the fascination with the spirit world is how little we know about it. It is important to keep that in mind and always play it safe. That doesn't mean if you're interested in EVPs you should avoid them but you should take anything you hear with a big grain of salt.

Stillwater Cemetery seems to be an EVP hotspot. Local ghost hunting hobbyists have spread the word that, if you are looking for some EVPs, this is the place to go. Surprisingly some of the voices on multiple tapes, taken on completely different days by totally different groups, appear to contain some of the same voices. There is one male voice in particular that not only tends to show up often on Stillwater tapes but actually will respond to questions asked of him by the living. His voice has never been heard on site but it inevitably shows up later on when the tape is replayed. He is evasive when asked personal questions, if he has ever given anyone his name or the details of his life and death they haven't come forward to say so, but he likes to act as an invisible tour guide to the tombs and residents of the cemetery.

If you're interested in trying to get your own tape and guided tour all you need is some kind of recording device. You'll find experts pretty evenly split on whether digital or non-digital recorders are the best. Many feel that digital recorders pick up EVPs better than their non-digital counterparts but that it is easier for digital recordings to be manipulated by the living and so they are often regarded as being fraudulent. As long as you're trying to get a tape for your own purposes that doesn't really matter. EVPs are as likely to be gotten on a bright sunny afternoon as they are a dark Halloween night so there is really no good reason to trespass after dark. Simply turn your recorder on and begin to walk around. If you want to try and 'converse', throw a few questions out into the empty air and leave time for the spirits to answer. Don't be discouraged if you don't hear a reply. You most likely won't until you're home and replay the tape.

It can be tough to gather EVPs outside because, of course, it will not be as quiet as it would be in an empty house. Recordings at Stillwater Cemetery will probably contain the background noise of traffic, lawnmowers running, and barking dogs. But there is always the possibility you might pick up voices that have no business being there.

Troy

Troy's nickname as 'the Collar City' is a holdover of the days when this historic city was home to more than two dozen textile factories that specialized in shirt cuff and collar manufacturing. Like many cities that originally depended on textiles as a main source of income Troy has faced some economic challenges. In recent years the city has, for the first time, tried to restore and protect what remains of the historic buildings that managed to survive some pretty indiscriminate bull dozing in the 1970's. It is also working hard to encourage small businesses to start up in the area and residents have seen an influx of small boutiques, art galleries, and the introduction of restaurants featuring dishes from just about any part of the world you can name.

Troy, despite its sort of traditional factory town roots, has a quirky history. Famous Troy residents have included Herman Melville, the world famous madam Mame Faye, Kurt Vonnegut, the inventor of the Ferris wheel, and Jane Fonda.

Frear Park

Originally Bradley and Wright Lakes were the water supply for the city of Troy. But the city grew faster than anyone had first expected and soon the two small lakes were not enough to supply the entire town. As time passed other bodies of water were developed for drinking water and eventually Troy abandoned the waterworks at Bradley and Wright Lakes. Troy citizens soon started a campaign to make the area around the lakes a public park and by the early 1890s the state of New York granted the city permission to do just that. The project would lag for another twenty-five years until the Frear family donated a huge tract of surrounding land towards the park project. This brought the final acreage count up to 112 acres. Over the next few years the Frears and other important local families would all donate more land, finally creating a park that had over one hundred and fifty acres of land for public use. In time golf courses, tennis courts, playgrounds, picnic spots, and even an ice hockey rink would all be added to Frear Park.

Distinguished Troy families donated the land needed to create this public park around the towns old water reservoirs.

There have long been stories about the park, some will say ghost stories, others will say the stories are linked to something much more frightening. People who have parked their cars in the park late at night have been astonished to feel a great weight jump onto, or bump heavily into, their car. Many of the people who have experienced the frightening occurrence find scratches that look as though they could be claw marks in the paint the next day. While many have seen an enormous dark shape causing the disturbance not one witness has gotten a clearer look at the vandal.

The golf course was added after the park was built. Some people have had frightening experiences in Frear Park at night.

The dark shape is inevitably described as being far too large to be a person. This has led to some speculation that there is some kind of unexpected, or previously unidentified, animal living in and around the park. It seems like a wild theory but it makes a great deal of sense to anyone who has been held captive in their vehicle while something unknown claws the back. Other people give the disturbance a ghostly cause, saying the damage is caused by some kind of inexplicable dark energy force. Why it would be drawn to cars and only at night is debatable.

Is some kind of wild animal or a dark force damaging cars in Frear Park?

John

A popular local legend in Troy involves a long ago teacher, only known as John after all this time has passed, and an axe. Depending on who's telling the story John was a teacher in either 1900 or 1936 that went berserk and killed some of his students in room 243 with an axe. The stories go on to say that you can still to this day hear the sound of children playing in that room and that sometimes even old axe wielding John makes an appearance.

The stories about axe murderer John seem to be another case of legends tangling as time passes. The big debate isn't *if* the school is haunted but *which* school is haunted. Various version of the story place it in the current Lansingburgh High School, an old Lansingburgh school building or the building that once housed Lansingburgh Academy that is now the Lansingburgh location of the Troy Public Library.

Forest Park Cemetery

In 1923 Nobel Prize winner Charles Richet coined the term *ectoplasm*. Richet, a French physiologist, had a variety of 'hobbies' and the bibliography of his works includes books on neurochemistry, psychology, history, medicine, sociology, poetry and the theater arts. Hyper-intelligent, incessantly curious, and a true man of his times it is, perhaps, not surprising that a scientist like Richet would become so interested in the spiritualist movement that gripped the United States during his lifetime. As he grew older he moved away from the hard sciences and became more and more interested in what today we would call parapsychology and paranormal studies.

Richet became friends with the most famous mediums and occultists of his day. In 1905 he would become the President of England's Society for Psychical Research, and later would be

President of Paris's Institut Metapsychique International. During his time as President of these research groups he would be credited with coining the word *metapsychics*, along with *ectoplasm*.

Ask the average American about ectoplasm and they will probably talk about Slimer from the *Ghostbusters* movies. Most people picture ectoplasm as a green to yellow mucus like material. This popular vision of ectoplasm is not entirely wrong; there have been some very rare cases of ectoplasm emissions that resemble slime. But the most credible and frequent reports of ectoplasm describe a mist or a diaphanous, gauze like material. Ectoplasm is also most commonly gray to white in color, not the Technicolor bright green popularized in movies. It is moist, cold to the touch, and is often described as having the scent of burning ozone.

Richet experimented a great deal with ectoplasm and found that it exists in different states throughout three separate stages. In its earliest state the human eye cannot see it. In more modern time there has been some success in photographing ectoplasm in this state using infrared technology. In ectoplasms second stage it is most identifiable. It is a moist, dense, vaporous liquid. In its final stage, Richet tells us, the liquid has evaporated from the ectoplasm and it becomes gauzy, like a mass of cobwebs or gossamer strands.

Ectoplasm is a material secreted from the bodies of physical mediums. Physical mediums are thought to be the most rare of all the wild talents. While in a deep trace like state ectoplasm rises or pours from the body of the physical medium. At this point it may form the face or part of the body of a spirit. Ectoplasm is extremely sensitive to light. Even just the glow from a flashlight can cause it to retreat back into the mediums body, sometimes with enough force to cause bruises. In some cases mediums have been injured when harm was caused to the ectoplasm still connected to their bodies. In a few uncommon, and highly disputed cases, bystanders to ectoplasm events have reported feeling ill after coming in contact with the substance.

There are a few different theories regarding what purpose ectoplasm actually serves. Some people believe that it is a subconscious formation created on the part of the medium, like an effort by the mediums body to materialize the spirit they are conversing with. Others feel it is a manifestation of the symbiotic relationship between the medium and the spirit. In this theory the medium creates the ectoplasm for the sole purpose of allowing the spirit to drape the ectoplasm over its body, thus allowing the spirit to interact with our plane of existence. Since most physical mediums have shown varying degrees of telekinesis, thought to be the most powerful of all the psychic powers, it has also been theorized that ectoplasm is the spiritual energy that makes psi talents possible.

Psychic powers, telekinesis, medium ship, and ectoplasm itself have all been resoundly rejected by the established scientific community. Of these ectoplasm is probably the least well regarded. In part this is because of the enormous rarity of ectoplasm occurrences. There simply haven't been enough of them in controlled settings for science to take them seriously enough to warrant further investigation. But the biggest problem facing those trying to validate ectoplasm is the sheer number of hoaxes that have been perpetrated by con artists passing themselves off as physical mediums. Many impressive ectoplasm displays have later been found to be combinations of egg whites, cheesecloth, and muslin.

Richter was not the only scientist to become fascinated with ectoplasm. Between 1908 and 1913 Dr. Albert von Schrenck-Notzig studied paranormal phenomena. He had a specific interest in ectoplasm. Dr. Von Schrenck-Notzig is most famous for the work he did with Eva Carriere, the notable French psychic. Eva Carriere could manifest ectoplasm from her mouth, nose, and ears at will and even emanated beams of light from between her fingers on some occasions. Carriere was studied by all of the great scientists of her age and most of them publicly declared their belief that she was the source of an otherworldly substance they could not explain. Sir Arthur Conan Doyle, of Sherlock Holmes fame, studied her performances under the watchful gaze of Dr. Von Schenck-Notzig and was an ardent believer that her performances were genuine. Harry Houdini, the great séance skeptic, was not so easily convinced. He was never able to offer actual proof that Carriere was a hoaxer but he thought she was relying on precisely the same magician's tricks of misdirection that he used himself when onstage.

As rare an occurrence as ectoplasm events are these days that does not mean they don't sometimes crop up in surprising ways. One night Chris and two of his friends hopped the gate at Forest Park Cemetery to see if the stories about the place were true. A friend of theirs from school swore that he himself had seen statues crying and they wanted to see if they would see something similar. They didn't see any of the ghosts that are normally associated with this place but what they did experience was, possibly a much rarer paranormal event.

Chris felt extremely cold, no surprise there since it was late fall, and it was even less surprising that the chill felt worse around his exposed neck. It wasn't until a friend walked up asking Chris were he got the weird scarf that he started to realize something very strange was going on. Turning his head slightly he could see, just barely in his peripheral vision, a gauzy dirty white material draped around the back of his neck. Thinking it was some kind of joke his friend reached out to pull the 'scarf' from him but Chris's sudden cry of pain stopped him immediately. Then the boy noticed the scarf seemed to be growing. Afraid the two teens ran, leaving Chris alone in the cemetery and with no ride home.

It was the least of his worries. Chris was as freaked out by the strange film around his head as his friends were, but the sudden bolt of pain he received when his friend had touched it deterred him from trying to remove it himself. He started to run. By the time he made it home there were only a few scraps of something indefinable and dirty looking clinging to his fall coat. Chris's friends avoided him like the plague after that and he tried desperately to forget the incident. It wouldn't be until years later, when he happened to catch a documentary about early 20th century spiritualism on TV, that he was able to give a name to the strange occurrence.

Chris had no interest in the paranormal and was certainly not interested in developing the latent talent he appeared to have as a physical medium. Even years later he felt squeamish talking about the incident. A few other witnesses to the strange events in Forest Park Cemetery over the years have claimed to see ectoplasm pouring from the statues that supposedly cry.

More than anything Chris's story illustrates just how unusual some of the paranormal encounters inside Forest Park Cemetery can be. Unfortunately the unusual encounters are not enough for some ghost story aficionados. You will find a host of mis-information associated with this place that does seem, once you dig past some more ridiculous urban legends, to be truly haunted in its own right.

In the Capital District you can find otherwise serious ghost hunters who will repeat the most common and widespread of American urban legends, placing them in Forest Park. This includes some of the oldest yarns out there. Like the teenagers who go to park in the cemetery but their amorous plans are interrupted by a scratching at the roof of the car. When they go to investigate they find the toenails of a hanged man dragging across the roof were causing the noise. Even as recently as 1996 a cab driver swore to the Troy Record that he picked up a fare at Emma Willard who asked to be brought to a Pinewood address. As they passed the cemetery the 'girl' disappeared from the cab without paying or opening her door. Other persistent stories are that the cemetery contains one of seven gates into Hell and that it sits above a forgotten older graveyard, most likely of Native American origin. There has been no evidence of previous burials in Forest Park, no bones or funeral trinkets found as new graves were dug, which is not to say that there could not have been a former cemetery. But it makes it unlikely. Gates leading to Hell seem as obviously fictitious as escaped psychopaths with hooks for hands mauling teenagers, which is yet another urban legend that, in the Capital District at least, seems to get set in Forest Park Cemetery more than any other spot.

But none of that is to say that there aren't some real, or at least far more likely, haunting going on in the cemetery. The story that drew Chris and his friends to the cemetery to begin with, the story of the crying statues, is very popular and has been told since the cemetery began. There are multitudes of these reports, some going so far as to say that the statues cry blood. Today if you visit the grounds you'll find most of the statues are headless, apparently the work of vandals who are drawn to them by the stories. Crying babies are often heard when the cemetery is otherwise empty and many visitors complain of feeling watched or followed as they walk the grounds. More than a few have felt icy hands grip their own as they walked amongst the graves.

Even with all of the real ghost stories that take place here what Forest Park Cemetery enthusiasts consider its real claim to fame is that it was named in a Life Magazine Top 10 list of most haunted places in America. Sadly that seems to be just another persistent myth. While you can find many newspaper articles and books that repeat news of its placement in the Top 10 list it is unclear precisely where they got the idea in the first place. Life Magazine's archives reveal no such inclusion. Nor do Time Magazine's archives, another magazine that is mentioned, though much less frequently than Life, as the source of Forest Parks 'Top Ten' status. Archives are often not as complete as they should be, especially since sources have dated the supposed article anytime from the 1950s to the 1970s, but the magazines 'morgue departments', as the archival rooms are called, show neither the article nor a missing issue that would have held the article. It appears the 'claim to fame' is simply one of those things that have been repeated so many times, over so many years, that no one has bothered to check and see if it's true.

The Troy Country Club

The back entrance of the Troy Country Club runs alongside Forest Park Cemetery and a dozen or so of the graves that were once part of the cemetery now lie on land owned by the country club, so it is of little surprise that there are almost as many ghost stories associated with this place as there are with Forest Park! You will hear many tales that are very similar to those attached to Forest Park Cemetery, stories so similar the Troy Country Club probably wouldn't even be worth mentioning at all if it wasn't for their additional haunting, a ghostly waitress.

One winter in the 1970s, a waitress was speeding up Pinewood Avenue, trying to get to the Troy Country Club in time for her work shift. The combination of speed on icy roads and poor visibility from the snowstorm proved fatal. Since then, during the winter months at least, you can see the misty image of the waitress walking around in the snow as if trying to find her way through a blizzard to get to work. Some people have even found footprints, created by the small feet of a woman, in the snow around the country club. They begin out of nowhere and fade away before getting anywhere in particular.

Rensselaer Polytechnic Institute

Rensselaer Polytechnic Institute is the oldest technological university in the country. It is known for providing an education strong in the sciences and technologies. So many people are surprised to learn that some of the very scientific minds that have passed through these halls over the years walk away convinced that something paranormal was sharing their school with them.

West Hall is RPI's most haunted location. This is none to surprising considering the age of the building and the variety of uses it has been called upon to house over the years. Originally West Hall was Troy Hospital. Up until this point the medical facilities in the city where in churches, temporary buildings, or church run orphanages. The construction of this new permanent hospital was meant to revolutionize healthcare for the residents of Troy. It would remain a hospital building until 1914 when it was deemed to be no longer suitable to meet the needs of the city due to its age and size. Until the building was purchased by RPI it was used as Troy's Catholic Central High School.

The buildings varied uses over the years can be seen in the rooms to this day. One room that housed a museum for RPI, for example, was once gymnasium that had previously been the operating theater. West Hall, under RPIs ownership, housed the schools geology department until 1998 when the building, located father away from the central campus than any other building, was converted to office use. Today few classes are actually held here.

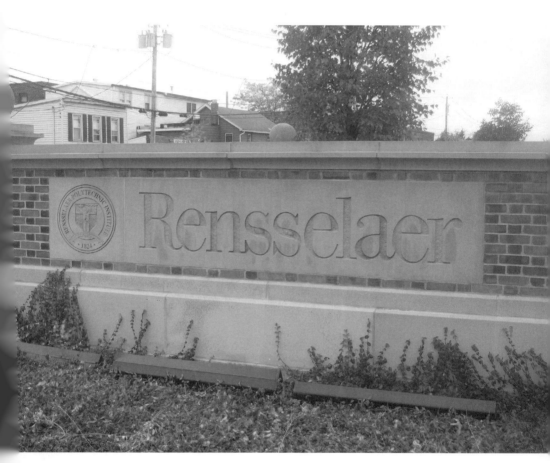

RPI is the oldest technological school in the country- and is
home to some very old ghosts!

One of the more active spirits that can found is Betsy, a nurse dating from the earliest days of the hospitals construction. She has been seen or sensed on all floors of the building, with the exception of the sub-basement. She appears in her old fashioned but still crisp white nurse's uniform. Betsy seems to simply be curious about the people that come into West Hall. She is not seen as a scary ghost or even as a protective one. The periods of renovations that have been completed in West hall have neither agitated her nor pleased her. Legend says that Betsy died while trying to save the children in the hospital, during a fire that caused extensive damage to the building when it was still the Troy Hospital.

Over the years RPI has allowed several ghost hunting groups to come in and investigate. Every one has walked away with information that leads them to believe this is a very haunted building. Most teams have gone in with tape recorders and cameras, and each one has walked away with a plentitude of orb photographs and EVPs. The ghosts in West Hall seem eager to converse with the living as much as they possibly can. It is interesting to note that for all of the voices that have appeared on EVPs taken in West Hall over the years none of them have purported to be the ghost of Betsy.

Afterword

In many ways *Ghosts of New York's Capital District* has been a way of coming full circle for me. My childhood was spent in Scotia, New York, and when I was growing up I had a special love for books chock full of true-life haunting. As a kid I could tell you stories of the history, murders, and haunting of far-off locales, but I don't think I could have told you one that took place in upstate New York. I remember always being disappointed when I went to the local library or bookstore and couldn't find even one book that discussed specifically at the places I knew so well.

Whether you decide that the stories in this book are evidence of life after death, are an interesting look at the parts of local history that oftentimes get left out of the history books, or as simply entertaining ghost stories to tell around the campfire that maybe hit a little closer to home because they are set in your own town is entirely up to you.

Bibliography

Betancourt, Marian. "Historic Saratoga Springs Inn is Home to Irish-American "Spirits"'. Travellady.com. March 2006.

Corbett, Theodore. *The Making of American Resorts: Saratoga Springs, Ballston Spa, and Lake George.* Fredericksburg, Pennsylvania: Rutgers University Press, 2001.

Dennett, Preston. *UFOs Over New York: A True History of Extraterrestrial Encounters in the Empire State.* Atglen, Pennsylvania: Schiffer Publishing, 2008.

Hart, Alan. *Dear Old Scotia.* Scotia, New York: Old Dorp Books, 2004.

Macken, Lynda. *Adirondack Ghosts.* New Jersey: Black Cat Press, 2000.

Marquis, Robyn. "Ghost Hunters Search West Hall for Spirits" *Polytechnic Online.* Troy, New York. October 22, 2008.

Obie, Julianna. "Spooky Schenectady" *Pheonix*. Schenectady, New York. October 2005.

Pitken, David J. *Haunted Saratoga County.* Chestertown, New York: Aurora Publications, 2005.

Pitken, David J. *New York State Ghosts: Volume 1.* Chestertown, New York: Aurora Publications, 2006.

Revai, Cheri. *Haunted New York: Ghosts and Strange Phenomenon of the Empire State.* Mechanicsburg, Pennsylvania: Stackpole Books, 2005.

Roberts, Nancy. *Civil War Ghost Stories and Legends.* Columbia, South Carolina: University of South Carolina Press, 1992.

Rusnica, Jennifer. "Is a Gate of Hell in Troy?" *Phoenix.* Schenectady, New York, October 2005.

Schlosser, S. E. *Spooky New York: Tales of Hauntings, Strange Happenings, and Other Local Lore.* Guilford, Connecticut: Globe Pequot Press, 2005.

Skinner, Charles Montgomery. *Myths & Legends of Our Own Land: Volume One.* Boston, Massachusetts: Adamant Media: December 2001.

Smitten, Susan. *Ghost Stories of New York State.* Auburn, Washington: Lone Pine Publishing, 2004.

Stone, Shawn. "Spa City Confidential" Metroland Online, www.Metroland.net, 2003.

Stone, William L. *Reminiscences of Saratoga and Ballston.* New York, New York: R. Worthington, 1880.

The following websites were instrumental in researching *Ghosts of the ol District:*

AlbanyRuralCemetery.org

GhostResearch.org

GraveAddiction.com

HistoricCherryHill.org

RPI.edu

Shadowlands.com

UFOEvidence.org

Union.edu

UnsolvedMysteries.com

Wikipedia.org

Yaddo.org

Index